# THE BEST OF A. B. SIMPSON

# *The Best of A. B. Simpson*

COMPILED BY

KEITH M. BAILEY

CHRISTIAN PUBLICATIONS

*Camp Hill, Pennsylvania*

Christian Publications
3825 Hartzdale Drive, Camp Hill, PA 17011


The mark of vibrant faith


ISBN: 0-87509-314-0
LOC Catalog Card Number: 86-72008
© 1987 by Christian Publications
All rights reserved
Printed in the United States of America


All excerpts taken from books by A. B. Simpson,
published by Christian Publications.

# CONTENTS

# INTRODUCTION

AMONG THE EVANGELICAL leaders living at the close of the 19th century, none was more dynamic and creative than Albert Benjamin Simpson—the founder of The Christian and Missionary Alliance. In 1881, Simpson resigned the pulpit of the fashionable and wealthy Thirteenth Street Presbyterian Church in New York City to pioneer a concept of church life that differed from the stereotypes and encrustations of Protestant denominationalism prevalent in his time. Simpson had found new wine and sought new wineskins to contain it.

Little did he dream that the small independent congregation he started by faith would become the mother of a worldwide missionary movement and a vital denomination in North America. The church he founded did not remain small. He was soon preaching to large crowds and his Gospel Tabernacle became a center for evangelism in the New York City metropolitan area.

Even before founding the Gospel Tabernacle, Simpson had been convinced of the need for literature that would lucidly set forth his burden for world evangelism as well as his emphasis on the fullness of Christ. Prior to leaving the Presbyterian church, he had flaunted all tradition by publishing a pictorial missionary magazine—the first of its kind in the history of the church.

Simpson did some of his best writing as editor of the magazines he published. Those publications were the forerunners of the *Alliance Life* (formerly *The Alliance Witness*), the official magazine of The Christian and Missionary Alliance. The articles and editorials in *The Word, The Work and The World* and *The Christian Alliance* provide some of the best examples of his writing style.

Formal theological training and years of diligent study gave Simpson a wealth of material for his productive years as a writer. His worldwide travels and his knowledge of literature, the classics, history and world affairs further equipped him to write. Simpson drew freely from his literary background and made his sermons and books come alive with well-chosen illustrations.

Simpson did much of his writing while pastoring a large city church, as well as serving as an administrator, teacher, conference speaker and publisher. He had little time to devote to the detail and contemplation of the scholars. What Simpson wrote was the overflow from a busy but dedicated life. It was a message crying out from the depth of his soul. Albert Simpson was a practitioner and his writings reflect that perspective.

Nevertheless, A. B. Simpson was a pietist and a mystic. His emphasis on the centrality of Christ captivated even his strongest critics. Those who differed most with some of his doctrine and practice held him in high regard as a man of God. Yet at the same time, he was a pragmatist. He lifted the reader into the heavenlies, but not for one moment did he neglect the practical outworking of life in Christ.

Simpson had a gift for making Scripture come alive. Though sensitive to doctrinal accuracy, he stated theology in non-technical language. He made spiritual concepts live for both the layman and the theologian.

Though the writings of Simpson reflect a broad knowledge of systematic theology, he did not write with the precision of the theologian. He was not bound by any closed system of theological thought. Simpson had been educated in the reformed theology of the Presbyterian church, but he showed remarkable openness toward the concepts of Arminian theology.

Simpson, however, drew from more than formal training and personal interest. He testified that from the time he was filled with the Spirit, he acquired a marked new ability to write both poetry and prose. Simpson had the soul of a poet and even his prose was prone to reach for high levels of inspiration. Hymns, pamphlets, articles and books flowed from his pen. He covered a wide range of doctrinal subjects and almost every book of the Bible.

Simpson was not afraid to confront the issues of his day. His published articles and books indicate a keen insight into the problems evangelicals faced at the turn of the century. He defended the gospel with intelligence and candor and, having judged the situation rightly, paved the way for many innovations in the church.

He saw the danger of liberalism and courageously defended the faith. With equal zeal he spoke out against the paralyzing effect of dead orthodoxy. Simpson conceived of the church as filled with the Spirit and in action.

The consuming passion of Simpson's life and ministry was to awaken the church to the necessity of carrying out the Great Commission. From his perspective, the imminent coming of Christ demanded an urgent response to missionary action. Simpson was more optimistic regarding the church than many of his contemporaries. He saw Matthew 24:14 as applicable to the church age. He did not see the church in ruin at the end of the age, but rather impelled by a fresh outpouring of the Holy Spirit to speed the gospel to the ends of the earth.

The missionary burden that consumed Simpson was much more than rhetoric. He became a creative innovator of missionary methods. What Simpson wrote on the subject of overseas missionary outreach was practical. He laid tracks upon which a local church as well as the larger movement could practice world evangelism.

Simpson addressed the common man in all his writings. The lay reader was his audience, and he wanted to teach him the mandate of world missions and the provisions of spiritual energy for carrying it out.

Walter M. Turnbull, an authority on Simpson's life and writings, calculated that 80 volumes came from his pen. At least 2,000 of his sermons were put into print as were many tracts and pamphlets and over 100 hymns he composed.

The chapters in this collection make up what, in my judgment, are *The Best of A. B. Simpson*. They have been arranged under the major themes he so often addressed. I trust this book will introduce many readers to the rich ministry of A. B. Simpson.

Keith M. Bailey
First Alliance Church
Louisville, Kentucky

CHAPTER

1

# Himself

*"Himself" is the classic that best describes Albert B. Simpson's theology. The tract, "Himself," is the most widely read work of Simpson. The influence of this digest of his teaching on the indwelling Christ has gone across denominational lines and blessed untold thousands in every part of the world. The special appeal of "Himself" has been its sound and sane teaching on the Deeper Life. Its message of the sufficiency of Christ is timeless, attracting each new generation of readers with its freshness.*

LET ME FOCUS YOUR THOUGHTS on Jesus and Jesus only. Often I hear people say, "I wish I could get hold of divine healing, but I cannot." I hear others exclaim, "I have got it!" But when I ask, "What have you got?" they do not really know. Sometimes they answer, "I have got the blessing" or "I have got the healing" or "I have got sanctification."

I thank God it is not the blessing, not the healing, not the sanctification, not the *thing* or the *it* that we want, but Some*one* far better. We want Christ, Christ *Himself*.

5

## We need the Person

How often the expression occurs in the Word: "Himself took our infirmities and bare our sicknesses" (Matthew 8:17); "His own self bare our sins in his own body on the tree" (1 Peter 2:24). It is the person of Jesus Christ whom we want. Plenty of people get the idea, but they do not get anything out of it. They get *it* into their heads and their consciences and their wills, but somehow they do not get *Him* into their lives and spirits. They have only that which is the outward expression and symbol of the spiritual reality.

I once saw a picture of the Constitution of the United States very skillfully engraved in copper plate. When I looked at it closely, it was nothing more than a piece of writing. But when I stood back and looked at it, it was the face of George Washington. At a little distance, the face became evident in the shading of the letters and I saw the person, not the words or the ideas. Then it came to me: *That is the way to look at the Scriptures and understand the thoughts of God. We can see in them the face of love shining through the words. It is Jesus* Himself *as the Life and Source and sustaining Presence of all our life.*

I prayed a long time to get sanctified. Sometimes I thought I had *it*. On one occasion I felt something, and I held on with a desperate grip for fear I should lose *it*. I kept awake the whole night fearing *it* would go, and, of course, *it* went with the next sensation and the next mood. I lost *it* because I did not hold on to *Him*. I had been taking a little water from the reservoir when all the time I might have been bathed in the fullness of Jesus.

I went to meetings and heard people speak of joy. I even thought I had the joy, but I did not keep it because I had not Jesus Himself as my joy. At last Jesus said to me, oh, so tenderly, "My child, just take Me. Let Me be in you the constant supply of all this, Myself." At last I got my eyes off my sanctification and my experience of it and instead began gazing upon Christ Himself. Instead of an experience, I found Christ to be larger than the moment's need, the Christ who had all that I should ever need. And He was given to me at once and *forever*!

When I thus saw Him, it was reassuring rest. It was all right and right forever. I had not only what I could hold that little hour, but also in Him all that I should need the next hour and the next and the next. Sometimes God gives me a glimpse of what it will be like a million years from now when we shall "shine forth as the sun in the kingdom of [our] Father" (Matthew 13:43) and have "all the fulness of God" (Ephesians 3:19).

### Healing is the life of Christ

Similarly, in my ignorance I thought that healing would be an *it*. I thought that the Lord would take me, like the old run-down clock, wind me up and set me going again, much as He might recycle a machine. It was not so at all. I found it was Jesus *Himself* coming into my life, giving me what I needed at the moment.

I wanted to have a great stock of healing so that I could feel rich. I wanted to have a great store of healing laid up for many years so that I would not be dependent upon God the next day. But God never gave me such a store. I never have had more holiness or healing at one time than I needed for that hour. God said, "My child, you must come to Me for the next breath. I love you so dearly I want you to come all the time. If I gave you a great supply of health, you would do without Me and would not come to Me so often. Now you have to come to Me every second and rest in Me every moment."

God gave me a great fortune. He placed millions and millions at my disposal, giving me a checkbook and this one condition: "You never can draw more than you need at the time." Whenever I have needed to make a withdrawal, there is the name of Jesus on the check! My frequent requests have brought more glory to Jesus. They have kept His name before the heavenly world. And God has been glorified in His Son.

I had to learn to take my spiritual life from Jesus every moment, to breathe Himself in as I breathed myself out. So moment by moment for the spirit and moment by moment for the body we must receive. You ask, "Is not that a terrible bondage, to be always so dependent?" What? A bondage to be dependent on the One you love—your dearest Friend? Oh, no! It comes naturally, spontaneously, like a fountain, without consciousness, without effort. True life is always easy and overflowing.

And now, thank God, I have *Him*. I have not only what I have room for, but that which I have not room for, but for which I shall have room, moment by moment, as I go on into the eternity before me. I am like the little bottle in the sea, as full as it can be. The bottle is in the sea, and the sea is in the bottle. So I am in Christ, and Christ is in me. Besides that bottleful of ocean, there is a whole ocean beyond. While it remains in the ocean, that bottle can be filled over and over again.

## Christ must be our faith

The question for each of us then is not "What do I think of divine healing?" but "What do I think of Christ?"

"You were healed by faith," a friend once remarked to me.

"Oh, no," I objected. "I was healed by Christ." What is the difference? There is a great difference. There came a time when even faith seemed to come between me and Jesus. I thought I should have to work up the faith, so I labored to get faith. At last I thought I had it and that if I put my whole weight upon it, it would hold. I said, when I thought I had faith, "Heal me." I was trusting in myself, in my own heart, in my own faith. I was asking the Lord to do something for me because of something in *me*, not because of something in *Him*.

So the Lord allowed the devil to try my faith, and the devil devoured it like a roaring lion. I found myself so broken down that I did not think I had any faith. God allowed faith to be taken away to the point that I felt I had none.

And then God seemed to speak to me so gently, saying, "Never mind, My child. *You* have nothing, but I am perfect power, I am perfect love. I am faith, I am your life, I am the preparation for blessing and then I am the blessing, too. I am all within and all without and all in all forever."

It is to have "the faith of God," as Jesus exhorted His disciples (Mark 11:22, margin). "The life which I now live in the flesh I live—" not by faith *on* the Son of God, but—"by the faith *of* the Son of God" (Galatians 2:20, emphasis the writer's). That is it! It is not *your* faith or *my* faith. We have no faith in ourselves, any more than we have life or anything else in ourselves. We have nothing but emptiness. We must be open and ready to let Him do it all. We must take His faith as well as His life and healing and simply say, "I live by the faith of the Son of God."

My faith is not worth anything. If I had to pray for someone, I would not depend at all on my faith. I would say, "Here, Lord, am I. If you want me to be the channel of blessing to this one, just breathe into me all that I need." It is simply Christ — Christ alone.

## Have you yielded?

Is your body yielded to Christ for Him thus to indwell and work through? The Lord Jesus Christ has a body like yours, except that it is perfect. His is the body not of a man but of the Son of man. Have you considered why He is called the Son of man? The title means that Jesus Christ is the one typical, comprehensive, universal, all-inclusive Man. Jesus is the one Man who contains in Himself all that man ought to be, all that man needs to have. All the fullness of the Godhead and the fullness of perfect manhood has been embodied in Christ, and He stands now as the summing up of all that man needs. His spirit is all that our spirits need. His body possesses all that our bodies need. He has a heart beating with the strength that our hearts need. He has organs and functions redundant with life not for Himself but for humanity.

Jesus does not need strength for Himself. The energy that enabled Him to rise from the tomb above all the forces of nature was not for Himself. That marvelous body belongs to our bodies. We are members of His body. Our hearts have a right to draw from His heart all that they need. Our physical lives have a right to draw from His physical life their support and strength. It is not us, but it is the precious life of the Son of God.

Will you take Him as your life? You will not merely be healed, but you will have a new life for *all* your needs—a flood of life that will sweep disease away and remain a fountain of life for all your future need. Take Him in His fullness!

## My wonderful secret

If I were to announce that I had received from heaven a secret to wealth and success that God would give freely through me to anyone willing to accept it, your interest would be intense. I want to show you in God's Word a truth that is more precious. The inspired apostle Paul tells us that there is a "mystery which hath been hid from ages and from generations" (Colossians 1:26). It is a secret that the world has sought in vain, a secret wise men hoped they might find. God says it "is now made manifest to his saints." Paul went through the Roman world telling just this message to those who were able to receive it. Here it is: "Christ in you, the hope of glory."

Christ in you—this is the great secret. And I share it with you, if you will take it from God. It is a secret that has been wonderful to me! Years ago I went to God burdened with guilt and fear. I tried that simple secret, and it was the solution to all my fear and my burden of sins. Years passed, and I found sin overcoming me and temptation too strong to resist. I went to God a second time, and He whispered, "Christ in you!" and I had victory, rest and blessing.

## It wrought healing of the body

Then my physical body broke completely. I had always worked hard. From the age of 14 I studied and labored, sparing no strength. At 21 I took charge of a large congregation. Half a dozen times I broke down utterly. My constitution was worn out. Many times I feared I should drop dead in my pulpit. Because of a weakened heart and an exhausted nervous system, I could not ascend any height without a sense of suffocation.

I had heard about the Lord's healing, but I struggled against the thought. I was afraid of it. I had been taught in seminary that the age of the supernatural was past, and I could not go back on that early training. My head was in my way! At last I was brought to attend "the funeral of my dogmatics," as one person has termed it, and the Lord whispered again to me the little secret: "Christ in you!" From that hour I received *Him* for my body as I had received Him for my soul. I was made so strong and well that work has been a perfect delight.

Since that time, I have spent even my summer holidays in the hot city of New York, preaching and working among the masses. In addition, there has been the work of our home and college, an immense mass of literary work and much more besides.

But the Lord did more than remove my suffering. It was more than simple healing. He so gave me Himself that I lost the painful consciousness of physical organs. That is the best of the health He gives. I thank the Lord that He keeps me from all morbid, physical consciousness. This body of mine is no longer the object of anxious care. Jesus gives me life that is a delight, and my service for the Master is a rest and a joy.

## It brought quickening of the mind

Again, I had a poor sort of a mind, heavy and cumbrous. It did not think or work quickly. I wanted to write and speak for Christ. I wanted to have a ready memory so as to have the little knowledge I had gained always under command. I went to Christ about it and asked if He had anything for me in this way.

"Yes, my child," He replied, "I am made unto you wisdom." I had been always making mistakes, which I regretted, and then thinking I would not make them again. But Christ said that I might have His mind, that He would be my wisdom. He told me He could cast down imaginations and bring into captivity every thought to His obedience. He could make the brain and the head right. Then I took Him for all that. And since then, He has kept me from mental disability, and work has been rest.

I used to write two sermons a week, and it took me three days to complete one. But now, in connection with my literary work, I have numberless pages to write besides the conduct of very many meetings each week. All is delightfully easy to me. The Lord has helped me mentally, and I know He is the Savior of my mind as well as of my spirit.

I also had an irresolute will. I asked God, "Cannot You be a will to me?" He answered, "Yes, My child. 'It is God which worketh in you both to will and to do of his good pleasure.'" Then He taught me how and when to be firm and how and when to yield. Many people have a decided will, but they do not know how to hold on just at the proper moment.

I came to Christ as well for power for His work and all the resources for His service, and He has not failed me. And so I say, if this precious little secret of "Christ in you" will help you, you may have it. May you make better use of it than I! I feel I have only begun to learn how well it works. Take it and go on working it out, through time and eternity — Christ for all, grace for grace, from strength to strength, from glory to glory, from this time forth and even for evermore.

> Once it was the blessing, now it is the Lord;
> Once it was the feeling, now it is His Word.
> Once His gifts I wanted, now the Giver own;
> Once I sought for healing, now Himself alone.
>
> Once 'twas painful trying, now 'tis perfect trust;
> Once a half salvation, now the uttermost.
> Once 'twas ceaseless holding, now He holds me
>   fast;
> Once 'twas constant drifting, now my anchor's
>   cast.
>
> Once 'twas busy planning, now 'tis trustful
>   prayer;
> Once 'twas anxious caring, now He has the care.
> Once 'twas what I wanted, now what Jesus says;
> Once 'twas constant asking, now 'tis ceaseless
>   praise.
>
> Once it was my working, His it hence shall be;
> Once I tried to use Him, now He uses me.
> Once the power I wanted, now the Mighty
>   One;
> Once for self I labored, now for Him alone.

Once I hoped in Jesus, now I know He's mine;
Once my lamps were dying, now they brightly
   shine.
Once for death I waited, now His coming hail;
And my hopes are anchored safe within the veil.

# Christ Our Savior

*"Christ Our Savior" (from* The FourFold Gospel*) sets forth the first of four primary truths Simpson considered "gospel." Simpson understood salvation to be the work of God completely apart from human effort. In this study, he was especially concerned with initial salvation, but he was careful to view it in the context of complete biblical salvation. The death, resurrection and ascension of Christ provide the basis of God's offer of salvation to fallen men. The steps by which a person receives salvation are discussed in easy-to-read layperson's language.*

*And cried with a loud voice, saying, Salvation to our God which sitteth upon the throne, and unto the Lamb (Revelation 7:10).*

SALVATION IS THE cry of the ransomed around the throne when the universe is dissolving in wreckage and terror is filling the hearts of men. It is the first cry of the ransomed after they reach their home and have seen all that it means to be lost and to be saved, while the earth is reeling, and the elements are melting, and all things are quaking and trembling in the first approaches of the great catastrophe.

They see behind them all the way through which

the Lord has led them. Down that long vista they behold the toils they have come through and the perils they have escaped. They recognize how tenderly the grace of God has led them on and kept them safe. They see the robes and crowns that are prepared for them and all the joy of the eternal future which is opening before them. They see all this, and then they behold Him whose hand has kept it all safely for them, and whose heart has chosen it for them.

They look back upon all the past; they look forward into all the future; they look up into the face of Him to whom it was all due. And then they lift up their voices in one glad exultant cry: "Salvation to our God which sitteth upon the throne, and unto the Lamb." This is what salvation means; this is what they have believed for; this is what He died to give them. They have it all. They are saved and the full realization of it has come home to their hearts at last.

Let us look a little at what it means to be saved. It is not at all a little thing. We sometimes hear that certain Christians are *only* justified. It is a mighty thing to be justified. It is a glorious thing to be born again. Christ said it was greater to have one's name written in heaven than to be able to cast out devils. What does salvation mean?

## What we are saved from

1. Salvation takes away the guilt of sin. It frees us from all liability and punishment for past offenses. Sin deserves punishment. Salvation takes this all away. Is it not glorious to be saved?

2. Salvation saves us from the wrath of God. God hates evil and must punish it somehow. The wrath of

God is revealed from heaven against all unrighteousness of men. But salvation delivers us from this.

3. Salvation delivers us from the curse of the law. We can recall the terrors of the law's revealing, the lightning and thunder that surrounded the mountain and the terror of Israel before it was given at all. They could not bear that God should speak to them thus, and they entreated Moses, "Speak thou with us and we will hear; but let not God speak with us, lest we die."

But if the giving of the law was terrible, more terrible was its breaking. It is perilous to break the law of the land. The most tender appeal of affection does not avail to save the condemned criminal. Justice must be satisfied.

When the assassin of President Lincoln was stalking through the land, the law would have searched the world to find him. How terrible it must have been for him to feel that the eye of justice was looking for him and sooner or later would surely find him! The circle tightened and tightened around him till at last he was grasped in the cordon. So the cordon of law contracts around the sinner who is under its power. Salvation delivers us from this curse through Him who was made a curse for us.

4. It delivers us also from our evil consciences. There is always a shadow left on our hearts by sin and a feeling of remorse. It is the black wing of the raven, and its hoarse voice is ever whispering of despair. The memory of past guilt will follow people so that after many years they tell of crimes committed, the punishment for which they escaped, but the burden of which never left their consciences. Perhaps it seemed to slumber for a while, but at last it sprang upon them

like a lion. Salvation delivers us from our evil consciences. It takes the shadow from the heart and the stinging memory of sin from the soul.

5. It delivers us from an evil heart which is the source of all the sin in the life. It is natural for men to sin even while they hate it. The tendency toward evil is in every nature, chained to it like a body of death so that even when we want to do good, evil is present with us. It takes possession of the will and heart like a living death. It is offensive, it smells of the sepulcher, it is full of the poison of asps, it putrefies the whole moral being and bears it down to death. Salvation frees us from its power and gives us a new nature.

6. It frees us from the fear of death. It takes away the sting of that last enemy, through fear of whom we would otherwise all our lifetime be subject to bondage. I remember when I was a child what shock a funeral bell would give me. I could not bear to hear of someone being dead. The love of Christ has taken this all away. The deathbed of God's children is to them the portal of heaven.

7. Salvation delivers us from Satan's power and kingdom. God has "delivered us from the power of darkness and translated us into the kingdom of His dear Son." We are saved from the ills and the serpent and the bonds of sin, and the devil is a conquered foe. Salvation delivers us from much sorrow and distress in life. It brings a glorious sunlight into life and drives away those clouds of depression and gloom which overwhelm us.

8. Beyond all else, salvation delivers us from eternal death. We are not going down into outer darkness and the depths of woe. Christ has unlocked the fetters of the pit and saved us from endless death. We are deliv-

ered from that terrible agony which the kindest lips that ever spoke has called the "worm that dieth not, and the fire that is not quenched."

These are some of the things that salvation has delivered us from. Is it not indeed glad tidings?

## What salvation brings to us

1. Salvation bring the forgiveness of all our sins and entirely removes them. They are blotted out as completely as though we had paid all that was due for them, and they can never appear against us again.

2. Salvation brings us justification in the sight of God so that we stand before Him as righteous beings. We are accepted as though we had done everything He had commanded and had perfectly kept the law in every particular. With one stroke of the pen He erases the account that was against us; with another stroke He puts there all the righteousness of Christ.

We must accept both sides of this. The spotlessness of Jesus is put to our accounts as if it were our own. All His obedience to the Father is ours. All His patience and gentleness are ours. Every service that He has rendered to bless others is put to our accounts as if we had done it all. Every good thing we can discover in Him is ours, and every evil thing in us is His. That is salvation. Is it not wonderful?

3. Salvation brings us into the favor and love of God and secures for us full acceptance in the person of Jesus. He loves us as He loves His only begotten Son. The moment we are presented in the arms of Christ we are accepted in Him.

Dr. Currie, a brilliant Methodist writer and editor of one of the best journals of his church, dreamed one night that he died and went up to the gate of heaven.

There he met an angel and asked to be allowed to enter. The angel asked him who he was.

"I am Dr. Currie," he answered, "editor of the *Quarterly Review* of the Methodist Episcopal Church." The angel replied, "I don't know you; I never heard of you before." Soon he met another angel and told him the same story, and received the same answer: "I don't know you."

At last one of the angels said, "Let us go to the Judge and see if He will know you." He went before the throne and told the Judge about his life and the work he had done for the church, but received the answer from the Judge: "I don't know you at all." His heart was beginning to gather the blackness of despair, when suddenly there was One at his side with a crown of thorns upon His head.

"Father," this One said, "I know him. I will answer for him." And instantly all the harps of heaven began to sing: "Worthy is the Lamb that was slain," and he was ushered into all the glory of the celestial world. Not all the preaching we have done or all the service we have rendered will amount to anything there. We must be identified with the Man who wore the thorns; we must be accepted in the Beloved, and then the Father will love us even as He loves His Son. We shall stand with Him even as Christ does.

4. Salvation gives us a new heart. It brings to us regeneration of the soul. Every spark of life from the old polluted nature is worthless, and the divine nature is born in us as a part of our very being.

5. Salvation gives us grace to live day by day. A man may be pardoned and released from prison, but have no money to supply his needs. He is pardoned, yet he is starving. Salvation takes us out of prison and pro-

vides for all our needs besides. It enables us to rejoice in God, who "is able to keep [us] from falling, and to present [us] faultless before the presence of his glory with exceeding joy."

6. Salvation brings to us the help of the Holy Spirit, ever at our side as a gentle mother, helping our infirmities and bringing grace for every time of need.

7. Salvation brings to us the care of God's providence, causing all things to work together for our good. This is never true until we are saved; but when we are the children of God, all things in earth and in heaven are on our side.

8. Salvation opens the way for all the blessings that follow it. It is the steppingstone to sanctification and healing and the peace that passes understanding. From this first gateway the prospect opens boundlessly to all the good land we may go on to possess.

9. Salvation brings to us eternal life. It is, of course, only the beginning, but the heavenly land has its portals open even here. When we at last reach the throne and look out and see all the possibilities that yet lie before us, we shall sing with the ransomed, "Salvation to our God which sitteth upon the throne, and unto the Lamb."

## The process of these blessings

1. These blessings come through the mercy and grace of God. "God so loved the world, that he gave his only begotten Son, that whosoever believeth in him should not perish, but have everlasting life."

2. Salvation comes to us by the righteousness of Jesus Christ. He perfectly fulfilled every requirement of the law. Had He faltered in one temptation we could not have been saved. Think of that when you are

tempted to speak a hasty word. Suppose Jesus had done so. We could have been lost forever. Every moment He held steadfastly in the path of obedience, and His perfect grace and obedience are the price of our salvation.

3. Salvation comes to us through the death of Christ. His obedience is not enough. He must die. His crucifixion is the atonement for our sins.

4. Salvation comes through the resurrection of Jesus Christ from the dead, which was God's seal of His accomplished work and the pledge of our pardon.

5. Salvation comes through the intercession of Jesus at the right hand of the Father. He is our Great High Priest there, where He ever lives to make intercession for us, and thus keeps us in continual acceptance.

6. Salvation comes through the grace of the Holy Spirit. The Spirit of God is sent down, through the intercession of Christ, to carry out in our hearts and lives His work. He keeps our feet in the way, and He will never leave His work until He has put us forever into the bosom of Jesus.

7. Salvation comes to us by the gospel. It is presented to us through this message and our refusal to accept it, or our neglect to do so, fixes irrevocably, by our own act, our eternal condition. If we are saved, we become so by accepting the gospel, which is called "the gospel of your salvation."

## The steps to salvation

1. Conviction of sin is the first step. We must see our need and our danger before we can be saved. The Holy Spirit brings this to our heart and conscience. Until there is this knowledge of the need of Christ, He cannot be received; but when the heart is deeply

impressed under a sense of sin, Christ is precious indeed.

2. There must be next an apprehension of Jesus as our Savior. We must see Him as both able and willing to save. It will not do merely to feel and confess our guilt. We need to focus our eyes on Jesus. So Christ says to every seeking soul, "Look! Look! Look unto Me and be saved!" Every one which seeth the Son, and believeth on him, may have everlasting life."

3. Salvation comes by repentance. There must be a turning from sin. This does not consist of mere emotional feeling necessarily, but it does mean to have the whole will and purpose of heart turned from sin to God.

4. Salvation comes by coming to Jesus. We must do more than turn away from sin. That alone will not save us. Lot's wife turned away from Sodom—but she was not in Zoar. There must be a turning to Jesus as well as a turning from sin.

5. Salvation comes by accepting Jesus as the Savior. This does not mean merely crying out to Him to save, but claiming Him as the Savior, embracing the promises He has given, and so believing that He is our personal Redeemer.

6. Salvation comes by believing that Christ has accepted us and counting Him faithful who has promised. This will bring the sweetness of assurance and peace, and as we believe the promise, the Spirit will seal it to our hearts and witness that we are the children of God.

7. Salvation comes by confessing Christ as the Savior. This is a necessary step. It is like the ratification of a deed or the celebration of a marriage; it stamps and seals our act of commitment.

8. Salvation involves our abiding in Jesus. Having taken it for a fact, once for all, that we are saved, we must never do the work over again. "As ye have, therefore, received Christ Jesus the Lord, so walk ye in Him."

## What the Bible says about salvation

1. It is called God's salvation. It was not invented by man. God alone is the author of it, and He is the only Savior.

2. It is also called "your own salvation," because we ourselves must appropriate it.

3. It is called "the common salvation," because it is free to all who will accept it.

4. It is called a "great salvation," because it is full and infinite in its provisions. It is large enough for all our needs.

5. Christ is called the "mighty to save," because no matter how weak or how wicked we sinners may be, He is able to save us to the uttermost.

6. It is called a near salvation. "Say not in thine heart, Who shall ascend into heaven? (that is, to bring Christ down from above:) Or, Who shall descend into the deep? (that is, to bring up Christ again from the dead.) But what saith it? The word is nigh thee, *even* in thy mouth, and in thy heart: that is, the word of faith, which we preach; That if thou shalt confess with thy mouth the Lord Jesus, and shalt believe in thine heart that God hath raised him from the dead, thou shalt be saved" (Romans 10:6–9).

We do not have to get up into some exalted state to find Christ, or down into some profound and terrible experience. We can find Him everywhere we are. Salvation is at our door. We can take it as we find Him very near to us. No steps were allowed to God's ancient altar, for then some poor sinner might not be able to get up to it. Jesus is on the very plane where we are this moment. We can take His salvation here now. We can take Him as we are, and He will lead us into all the experiences we need.

## Why it is called the good news

1. It is called good news because of its value. It comes laden with blessings to us who receive it.

2. It is called good news because of its freedom. It may be taken without money and without price.

3. It is called good news because of its availability. It is easy of access, being on the level of the worst sinner.

4. It is called good news because of its universality. Whosoever will may take it and live.

5. It is called good news because of the security of its blessings. They are given forevermore. "Verily, verily, I say unto you, He that heareth my word, and believeth on him that sent me, hath everlasting life, and shall not come into condemnation" (John 5:24).

6. It is called good news because of the eternity of its blessings. The sun will have burnt itself into ashes, the earth will have been destroyed by intense heat, the heavens will be changed when salvation has only begun. Then a thousand times ten thousand years shall pass, and we shall have only begun a little to understand what salvation means. Blessed be God for the gospel of Christ's salvation.

## Why we should receive and share this salvation

1. Every man's salvation hinges upon his own choice and free will. It is an awful thing to have the power to

take salvation and to throw that opportunity away. And yet it is left to our choice. We are not forced to take it. We must voluntarily choose it or reject it.

2. The salvation of our souls is a tremendous responsibility for which we are held accountable. God has put salvation into our hands as a jewel of inestimable value, and He will hold us to a strict account for the way we treat this precious thing. If we destroy it, how fearful will be our doom when we meet the Judge of all the earth, and hear the stern question from His lips, "Where is thy soul?"

3. Guilt will rest upon us if we neglect and despise the precious blood of Christ shed for our salvation. To neglect it is to throw it away. He has provided a great salvation. If it is worth so much to man, if it has cost God so much to provide it, what can be thought of him who makes little of it? Jesus suffered intensely to bring salvation to us, and shall we stumble carelessly over it? Oh, let us be more concerned than we are, both for the salvation of our own souls and for those around us who are not saved.

4. The little word "now" is always linked with salvation. Salvation must be taken now or never. The cycle of life is very narrow. We do not know how soon it will end. "Behold, now is the day of salvation."

5. Salvation's issues are for eternity. The decisions there are not reversible. We cannot come back from death and have another chance to secure salvation. When once the Master has risen up and shut the door, we will find we have been left out forever. The cry will then be, "I have lost my chance; it is too late." God's Word holds out no second chance.

6. If salvation is missed there will be no excuse for it. Not one thing has been left undone in presenting

salvation to men. God's best thought and Christ's best love have been given to it. All has been done that could be done. Salvation has been brought down to our level. It has been placed where we can reach it.

God has provided all the resources, even the grace, repentance and faith, if we will take them. If we lack anything, God will put His arms around us and lift us up to Him, breathing His faith into us, and carrying us Himself until we are able to walk. Salvation is brought to every sinner. If we are lost it is because we have neglected and defied God's love.

Although we proclaim this salvation, eternity will be too short to tell it all. We must take it and then go out and gather others in to share it. We will receive glorious crowns, but the best of it all will be that men and women will be saved.

Hanging expensively framed in a New York city living room, is a little bit of paper—a telegraph form. On it is just one word: SAVED!

The cablegram was framed by the lady of that mansion, because it is dearer to her than all her works of art. One day when the awful news came to her through the papers that the ship on which her husband had sailed was wrecked, that little message came to her door and saved her from despair. It was the message of that rescued man, and it meant to two hearts all that life is worth.

Oh, let such a message go up today to yonder shore. The Holy Spirit will flash it hence while I am drawing the next breath. The angels will echo it over heaven, and there are dear friends there to whom it will mean as much as their own very heaven.

I have seen another short sentence in a frame, too. It came from one who had been rescued from a ship where friends and family had all perished. Those dear little ones were in the slimy caves of the cruel sea. Those beloved faces had gone down forever, but he was saved, and from yonder shore he sent back this sad and weary message: SAVED ALONE!

So I can imagine a selfish Christian entering yonder portals. They meet him at the gates. "Where are your dear ones?" "Where are your friends?" "Where is your crown?" "Alas, I am saved alone." God help you, reader, to so receive and give, that you shall save yourself and others also.

> *Must I go, and empty handed,*
> *Must I thus my Savior meet,*
> *Not one soul with which to greet Him,*
> *Lay no trophy at His feet?*

# 3

---

# Filled with the Spirit

*In "Filled with the Spirit" (from* The Larger Christian Life*), Simpson writes about the Spirit's work
within the believer subsequent to the new birth. The
book entitled* The Larger Christian Life *is made up of
sermons Simpson preached at the summer convention in
Old Orchard, Maine. This chapter relates the filling of
the Holy Spirit to the crisis of sanctification. To be filled
with the Spirit is to receive such an infilling of the Spirit
of Christ that one's spiritual, intellectual and physical
powers are all brought under the blessing and power of
the Holy Spirit. Simpson discusses the way the Spirit
makes the indwelling of Christ a reality in the believer.
He explains the conditions of heart and mind necessary
to receive such fullness.*

*Be filled with the Spirit (Ephesians 5:18).*

*Ye are complete [filled] in him (Colossians 2:10).*

THE EMPHATIC WORD in both Ephesians 5:18 and
Colossians 2:10 is "filled." It is the Greek *plaroo*
which means to fill full, so full that there will be no

space left empty. It does not mean to have a measure of the Holy Spirit and to be somewhat familiar with Christ, but to be wholly filled with, and possessed by, the Holy Spirit. It means to be utterly lost in the life and fullness of Jesus. It is the completeness of the filling which constitutes the very essence of the perfect blessing. A fountain half full will never become a spring. A river half full will never become a water power. A heart half filled will never know "the peace which passeth all understanding" and the power that flows from the inmost being as "rivers of living water."

## The nature of this filling

This filling is connected with a living Person. We are not filled with an influence, a sensation, a set of ideas and truths or a blessing. We are filled with a Person. This concept is entirely different from all other teaching. Human systems of philosophy and religion deal mainly with intellectual truths, moral conditions or external acts. Greek philosophy was a system of ideas; Confucianism is a system of morals; Judaism is a system of laws and ceremonies. Christianity is centered in a living Person, and its very essence is the indwelling life of Christ Himself. He is not only its Head and Founder but is forever its living Heart and Substance. And the Holy Spirit is simply the agent or channel through whom He enters, possesses and operates in the life consecrated to Him.

This reduces Christian life to beautiful simplicity. We do not need to fill up the various parts of our lives with many different experiences, ideas or influences. Rather, in the center of our being, we can simply receive Jesus in His personal life and fullness. Then He flows into every part of us and lives out His own life in all the diversified experiences and activities of our lives.

In one garden we plant the living seed and water it from the same great fountain, and lo, it springs up spontaneously with all the varied beauty and fruitfulness of the lily and the rose, the foliage plant and the fruit tree, the clinging jasmine and the spreading vine. We have simply to turn on the fertilizing spring and nature's spontaneous life bursts forth in all its beautiful variety.

This, by a simple figure, is Christ's procedure for the deeper life. Our being is the soil, He is the Seed, His Holy Spirit is the Fountain of Living Waters and "the fruit of the Spirit is love, joy, peace, long-suffering, gentleness, goodness, faith, meekness, temperance."

Out in the West lie millions of acres of barren land. They have great potential, but practically, they are fruitless and waste. Within the soil of these Saharas lie undeveloped riches, and all that is needed to bring them into fruitfulness is water. Let the mountain stream be turned into these deserts, let the irrigating channels spread their network over all these vast fields, and a lovely paradise results. The soil appears empty and barren, but fill it with seed, water it with springs, and then the transformation comes with spontaneous luxuriance.

So, too, the human heart is not self-constituted or self-sufficient. It is but a barren possibility. It may struggle its best to develop itself, but like the sagebrush and the stunted palms which cover the western deserts, it will develop only feebly. But drop into that heart the living Christ, and flood it with the water of the Spirit's fullness, and lo, it realizes its true ideal. The promise of Jesus' own simple parable is perfectly fulfilled: "He that abideth in me, and I in him, the same bringeth forth much fruit: for without me ye can do nothing" (John 15:5).

Shall we not realize, then, that God has made each of us, not as self-contained worlds of power and perfection, but simply as vessels waiting to be filled with Him? We are shells to hold His fullness. We are soil to receive His Living Seed and fertilizing streams, and to produce, in union with Him, the fruits of grace.

Into His living Son God has poured all His fullness, so that "in him dwelleth all the fulness of the Godhead bodily." The Holy Spirit has now become the great reservoir and the irrigation system through which the fullness of Jesus flows into us.

There is nothing which God requires of us, or which we can ever need in life but what Christ can supply for us. We may have an exact provision for our every need by simply receiving Him. This is the meaning of that beautiful expression, "Of his fulness have all we received, and grace for grace. For the law was given by Moses, but grace and truth came by Jesus Christ" (John 1:16–17).

All other systems give us merely the ideas of things or the commandments or laws which require them of us. But Christ brings the power to realize them. He is Himself the reality and substance in our hearts and lives. He is the great Typical Man. But He is more than a pattern or a type, exhibiting what we ought to be, demanding our imitation. He is also the Living Head and Progenitor of the very life which He Himself exhibits, begetting it in each of us by an imparta-tion of His very being, reproducing Himself in us by the very power of His own life. Then by the Holy Spirit from His own being, He feeds and nourishes this life in us.

Christ's Person, therefore, is far more than a pattern. He is a power, a seed, a spring of Living Water, even the very substance and support of the life He requires of us.

This Person is the true fullness of every part of our life. The idea of filling implies universality and completeness. We are not filled unless we are filled in every part. This is just what Christ proposes to do in our full salvation.

He fulfills all the requirements of our salvation, all the conditions involved in connection with our redemption, reconciliation, justification. He takes the indictment against us and erases it with His own precious atonement, writing in His own blood, "Settled forever." He takes the broken law, He takes the sad and humiliating record of our failures, omissions and transgressions, and expunges it with His own perfect righteousness. He writes over all our record, "Christ is the end of the law for righteousness to every one that believeth" (Romans 10:4). "Accepted in the beloved" (Ephesians 1:6). "He hath made him to be sin for us, who knew no sin; that we might be made the righteousness of God in him" (2 Corinthians 5:21).

And so, "we are complete in him." "By one offering he hath perfected forever them that are sanctified" (Hebrews 10:14), and we are as fully saved as if we had never sinned.

Now, the important thing is to realize that this work is complete. We should enter into the fullness of Christ by recognizing ourselves as fully justified and forever saved from all past sin and transgression through the complete redemption of Jesus Christ. The lack of fullness in our subsequent experience is largely due to doubts and limitations which we allow to enter here. Christ's work for our redemption was finished, and when we accept it, it is a complete and eternal salvation.

*Christ's work fills the deeper need of sanctification.* He has provided for this in His atonement and in the resources of His grace. It is all wrapped up in Him and must be received as a free and perfect gift through Him alone. "Of him are ye in Christ Jesus, who of God is made unto us . . . sanctification" (1 Corinthians 1:30).

Is sanctification the death of the sinful self? That life has been crucified with Him already upon the cross. We have but to hand it over to Him in unreserved committal, and He will slay it and bury it forever in His grave. Is sanctification a new life of purity, righteousness, peace and joy in the Holy Spirit? Still more emphatically, Christ Himself must be our life, our peace, our purity and our full and overflowing joy.

*Christ is the fullness of our heart life.* There is no place so sacred to us as our affections. And there is no place so claimed by the great adversary of our souls and so impossible to regulate by our own power and will. But Christ will give us His heart as well as His Spirit. He will cause us to love God as He loves Him — with all our "heart and soul and strength and mind." He will cause us to "love one another even as he has loved us." How blessed it is that we have One who will fill all the delicate, infinitely difficult and varied requirements of these sensibilities and affections. They carry with them such a world of possibility for our own or others' weal or woe.

*Christ will fill all the needs of our intellectual life.* Our mental capacities will never know their full wealth of power and spiritual effectiveness until they become the vessels of His quickening life. These minds of ours must be laid at His feet as the censers which are to hold His holy fire. He will think in us, remember in us, judge in us. He will impart definiteness and clearness to our conceptions of truth. He will give us the tongue of fire, the illustration that both illuminates and melts, the accent and tone of persuasiveness and sympathy, the power of quick expression and utterance. He will see that we have the equipment to make us workmen and women "that needeth not to be ashamed, rightly dividing the word of truth" (2 Timothy 2:15).

But, of course, we must be diligent and give faithful attention to His wise and holy teaching. Then as He leads us in His work, we will at once see our own shortcomings and His full purpose for us. We must be taught of God, and teaching is sometimes very gradual. But "He will guide [us] into all truth," and "perfect that which concerneth" our education and preparation for His work. The mind that the Holy Spirit quickens and uses will accomplish results for God which all the brilliance of human genius and the scholarship of human learning can never approach.

*Christ will fill the needs of our body.* His body has been constituted, by the resurrection from the dead, as a perpetual source of energy, sufficient for every physical function and every test that comes in the pressure of human life. In a world where every step is beset with the elements of disease, suffering and physical danger, Christ is the true life of a redeemed body. His Holy Spirit is able so to quicken these mortal bodies, as He dwells within us, that they shall receive a supernatural vigor directly derived from our exalted Head.

*Christ will fill all the needs that arise in our secular callings and the circumstances of our daily lives.* There is not one of them that may not be recognized as coming from Him and meant to prove His all-sufficiency in some new direction. If we had the faith to see God in every circumstance, day by day, every chapter of life's history would be a new story. The romance of heavenly love would transform darkness into light, difficulty into triumph, sorrow into joy and the earthly into the heavenly. Through us Christ would manifest Himself in grace and power to innumerable witnesses who never hear of Him from a pulpit or read His story in the Bible.

*Christ will fill our capacities for happiness.* He is the fullness of our peace and joy. He is the true portion of the people He has created. Wholly filled with Him, there is no room for either care or fear.

*Christ will fill that fundamental need on which every other experience of His fullness depends, namely, the faith that receives Him.* This, too, is but the life of Christ within us. Our highest part in the life of faith is to so boldly abandon even our best efforts to trust God that we can receive the very faith of God and claim the "all things [that] are possible to him that believeth" (Mark 9:23).

To be filled with Christ is not only to be filled with divine life in every part, but it is to be filled every moment. It is to take Him into the successive moments in our conscious existence and to abide in His fullness. Christ is not a reservoir but a spring. His life is continual, active and ever passing on with an outflow as necessary as its inflow. If we do not perpetually draw the fresh supply from the living Fountain, we shall either grow stagnant or empty. It is, therefore, not so much a perpetual fullness as a perpetual filling.

True, there are periodic experiences of spiritual elation which are part of God's plan for our life in Christ and are designed, no doubt, to lift us to a higher plane of abiding union with Him. There are the Pentecosts and the second Pentecosts — the great freshets and floodtides — all of which have their necessary place in the spiritual economy. But there is the continual receiving, breath by breath and moment by moment, between those long intervals and more marked experiences. This daily supply is even more needful to spiritual steadfastness and health. God would have us alive to all His approaches and open to all the "precious things of heaven . . . the dew, and . . . the deep that coucheth beneath, . . . the precious fruits brought forth by the sun, . . . the precious things put forth by the moon, . . . the precious things of the earth and fulness thereof" (Deuteronomy 33:13). Then we will know there is no moment of existence and no part of our beings that does not draw some blessing from Him.

## The effects of the divine filling

This divine filling is the secret of holiness. There is a measure of the Holy Spirit's life in every regenerate soul, but it is when every part of our being is filled with His love and possessed for His glory that we are wholly sanctified. Even as the descending cloud on the tabernacle left no room for human Moses, so this divine fullness excludes from our lives the power of sin and self.

Would you have continual purity of heart and thought and feeling? Would you be entirely conformed to the will of God? "Be filled with the Spirit." Let the heavenly water flow into every channel of irrigation and by every garden bed and plant. Then the graces of your Christian life will be replenished by His grace and bloom like the garden of the Lord. Only abide in Him and let Him abide in you, and you will bring forth all the fruit of the Spirit.

This is the secret of happiness. A heart half full is only full enough to be conscious of its lack. It is when the cattle are filled that they lie down in green pastures. "These things have I spoken unto you, that my joy might remain in you, and that your joy might be full" (John 15:11).

It is the secret of power. The electric current can so fill a copper wire that it will become a channel to turn the great wheels of the factory. The swift river has power to run a score of factories along its banks, but it is simply because it is perpetually supplied with water. Only full hearts accomplish effectual work for God. Only the overflow of our blessing blesses others.

## Conditions for being filled

Christ has promised to fill the hungry. "Blessed are they which do hunger and thirst after righteousness; for they shall be filled" (Matthew 5:6). As you read these lines you may be longing for this experience and thinking with discouragement of how far short you fall. This deep desire is the very beginning of the blessing you seek. Already the Holy Spirit is at work preparing you for the answer to your cry. No person finds the fullness of Jesus as speedily as the one who is most deeply conscious of his or her failure and need. Thank God for that intense desire that will not let you rest short of His blessing.

An eastern caravan traveling across the desert once found itself without water. The accustomed fountains were dry and the oasis was a desert. An hour before sunset, the caravan halted, the members too exhausted and parched to continue on. Dismay was upon all faces and despair in all hearts. But one of the ancient men approached the sheik and counseled him to unloose two beautiful harts he was conveying home as a present to his bride. Left to themselves, they would scour the desert for water. The animals' tongues were protruding with thirst, their bosoms heaving with distress. But as they were led out to the borders of the camp and then set free on the boundless plain, they lifted up their heads and sniffed the air with distended nostrils. Then, with unerring instinct and a course as straight as an arrow, they sped across the desert. Swift horsemen followed close behind, and an hour or two later they returned with the glad tidings that water had been found. With shouts of rejoicing, the camp moved to the happily discovered fountains.

So God has put within us that instinct for the springs of living water. Thank God if you have this deep spiritual thirst for Him. Follow it as it leads you to the throne of grace to wait and cry and receive. Then you can comment in the words of Jacob, "Satisfied with favour and full with the blessing of the Lord" (Deuteronomy 33:23).

The empty are always filled. "He hath filled the hungry with good things" (Luke 1:53). "Blessed are they which do hunger and thirst after righteousness: for they shall be filled" (Matthew 5:6). "Having nothing and yet possessing all things" (2 Corinthians 6:10). This is the paradox of grace. We never can be filled until we have room for God. Every great blessing begins with a great sacrifice, a great severance, a great dispossessing. "He brought us out . . . that he might bring us in" (Deuteronomy 6:23).

Abraham must let Lot have his choice before he can have his full inheritance. Isaac must be offered on Mount Moriah before God can make it the seat of His future temple. Moses must let go the honors and prospects of his Egyptian princedom before he can receive his great commission, the lasting honor of his life work. So we must be emptied of self and the world before we can be filled with Jesus and the Holy Spirit.

Are we willing to be emptied? "Make the valley full of ditches," is still the prophet's command, and the "valley shall be filled with water" (2 Kings 3:16–17).

Are we in the valley of humiliation? Have we opened in the valley the deep ditches of need and conscious insufficiency? In proportion as we can say, "I am not sufficient," we shall be able to add, "my sufficiency is of God."

Have we tossed overboard not only the old pirate self-will and his crew of worldliness and sin but also all the cargo of our own strength, our own faith, our own religious experience? Have we made room for Christ to be our ALL and in all always? Do we habitually cease from ourselves in everything and thus make it necessary for God to assume the responsibility and supply the sufficiency?

The open heart shall be filled. God said to Israel, "Open thy mouth wide and I will fill it" (Psalm 81:10). We know what it is for the flower to open its petals to the sunlight, the dew and the refreshing shower. Often we are closed so tight with unbelief, doubt, fear and self-consciousness that we cannot take in the love which God is waiting to pour out. We know what it is to find people closed up and heart-bound. We become conscious at once of the repulsion and feel all the fountains of our love obstructed and rolled back again upon our own aching hearts. They cannot receive us. It is like the mother who found her long-lost son after years of separation, but the child did not recognize her. She tried to awaken his memory of her, pouring out the full tides of her bursting heart, but her attempts only met with the dull stare of strangeness and suspicion. Her heart broken in grief and disappointment, she wept and sobbed in agony.

God is pouring out His love to many a person who cannot, will not receive Him. He is unknown. His face is strange. He seems to have no avenue to the dulled sensibilities of the world-loving man or woman. God has cause to exclaim, "How often would I have gathered [you]. . . as a hen gathereth her chickens under her wings, and ye would not!" (Matthew 23:37).

I watched a man slowly die simply because he could not swallow more than a single grain of food or spray of moisture. Many a Christian's spiritual larynx is just as shrunken. Millions are starving to death in the midst of plenty because their hearts are not open to receive God. There must be the love that draws near and takes. There must be the faith that accepts and receives. There must be the quietness of spirit that stays open long enough to be wholly filled.

Again, we are filled by waiting upon the Lord in prayer—continued and persevering prayer. It was after His disciples had waited upon the Lord that they were filled with the Holy Spirit. Prayer is not only an asking but also a receiving. Many of us do not wait long enough before the Lord to get filled. You can take your breakfast in half an hour, but you cannot be filled with the Holy Spirit as quickly.

There should be seasons of special waiting upon the Lord for this very purpose. There should be a ceaseless abiding in the Lord for the quiet replenishing, moment by moment. The one may be compared to the great rainstorms that flood the river, and the other to the ceaseless moisture of the air and the morning and evening dews.

No child of God who, in a proper spirit and with an entire self-surrender and trust, waits upon Him for the full baptism of His Holy Spirit will ever be disappointed. God promises that we shall go forth from such seasons refreshed and overflowing with His love and life. Power and blessing will follow such seasons, both in our own life and in the lives of others. Service for God and for others is perhaps the most effectual condition of receiving continually the fullness of the Spirit. As we pour out the blessing, God will pour it in. Every blessing we have received from God is a sacred trust, and it will be continued only as we use it for Him.

Our salvation is not our own. It belongs to every perishing soul on the face of the globe who has not yet had the opportunity of receiving Jesus. Our sanctification—the fullness of Jesus—is a sacred trust to be shared with every Christian who has not yet discovered this blessing. Our healing belongs to some sufferer. Our every experience is adjusted to some person and will enable us to meet his or her need if we are but faithful to the opportunities of God's providence.

How clear a truth becomes to us when we are trying to tell it to others! How real the baptism of the Holy Spirit is when we are kneeling by another's side to claim it for that one! How the streams of Christ's healing flow through our very flesh as we are leading some poor sufferer into the truth! How the joy of our salvation swells as we see it spring up in the person we have just led to the fountain!

What fullness God longs to share with everyone who has room to receive and readiness to give!

"If any man thirst, let him come unto me, and drink. He that believeth on me, as the scripture hath said, out of his belly shall flow rivers of living water" (John 7:37–38). As we have received His fullness, let us pass it on, drinking as the living waters flow through our hands. Then we shall realize in some measure the largeness and blessedness of that great promise of the Lord.

# Wholly Sanctified

*"Wholly Sanctified" (from the book by the same title) emphasizes another aspect of the Spirit-filled life. This chapter is adapted from a sermon Simpson preached from his own pulpit in March of 1890. The experience of sanctification comes not from man's own spiritual struggles, but is the direct work of Christ, the author of sanctification. The entire personality of the believer needs to be sanctified. Holiness produces completeness in the redeemed sinner. The practical outworking of full surrender to Christ the Sanctifier is a true separation from sin and self.*

*And the very God of peace sanctify you wholly; and I pray God your whole spirit and soul and body be preserved blameless unto the coming of our Lord Jesus Christ. Faithful is he that calleth you, who also will do it (1 Thessalonians 5:23–24).*

THE PROMINENCE GIVEN to the subject of Christian holiness, along with the revival of the doctrine of the Lord's Second Coming, is one of the signs of the times. The very opposition which these two subjects have received and the deep prejudice with which they are frequently met, emphasize more fully the force with which they are impressing themselves on the minds of our generation and the heart of the church of God. The only way we can know the direction of the weather vane is by the force of the wind. The stronger the wind blows against it, the more steadily it points in the true direction. So, too, the gales of controversy indicate the intense interest with which God's people are reaching out for a higher and deeper life in Him. They are somehow feeling the approach of a crisis in the age in which we live.

These two truths are linked closely together in the passage cited above. The former is the preparation for the latter, and the latter the complement of the former. Let us turn our attention, then, to the explicit teachings of this passage respecting the scriptural doctrine of sanctification.

## The Author of sanctification

The name God of Peace implies that it is useless to look for sanctification until we have been reconciled to God and have come to know Him as the God of peace. Justification—a justification so thoroughly accepted as to banish all doubt and fear and make God to us "the very God of peace"—is indispensable to any real or abiding experience of sanctification.

Is this perhaps the secret cause of our failure in reaching the higher experience for which we long? "If the foundations be destroyed, what can the righteous do?" (Psalm 11:3). Are there cracks or loose stones in the foundation of our spiritual lives? Is it necessary for us to lay again the solid groundwork of faith in the simple Word of Christ and the finished work of redemption? Then let us do so at once. Accept without feeling, without question, in full assurance of faith, the simple promises, "He that believeth on the Son hath everlasting life" and "Him that cometh to me I will in no wise cast out." Then take your stand on the Rock of Ages and begin to build the temple of holiness.

The expression "the very God of peace" further suggests that sanctification is the pathway to a deeper peace, even the "Peace of God which passeth all understanding." Justification brings us peace *with* God, sanctification the peace *of* God.

The cause of all our unrest is sin. "The wicked are like the troubled sea, when it cannot rest, whose waters cast up mire and dirt. There is no peace, saith my God, to the wicked" (Isaiah 57:20–21). But on the other hand, "Great peace have they which love thy law: and nothing shall offend them" (Psalm 119:165). So we find God bewailing His people's disobedience and saying, "O that thou hadst hearkened to my commandments! then had thy peace been as a river, and thy righteousness as the waves of the sea" (Isaiah 48:18).

Sanctification brings the soul into harmony with God and the laws of its own being, and there must be peace. Peace cannot be experienced in any other way. Moreover, sanctification brings into the spirit the abiding presence of the very God of peace Himself, and our peace is then nothing less than the deep, divine tranquility of His own eternal calm.

But the deeper meaning of the passage is that sanctification is the work of God Himself. The literal translation of this phrase would be "the God of Peace himself sanctify you wholly." It emphatically expresses His own direct personality as the Author of our sanctification. It is not the work of man or means or of our own strugglings. It is His own prerogative. It is the gift of the Holy Spirit, the fruit of the Spirit, the grace of the Lord Jesus Christ, the prepared inheritance of all who will enter in, the great obtainment of faith, not the attainment of works. It is divine holiness, not human self-improvement or perfection. It is the inflow into man's being of the life and purity of the infinite, eternal and Holy One, bringing His own perfection and working out in us His own will. How easy, how spontaneous, how delightful this heavenly way of holiness!

Surely it is a "highway" and not the low way of man's vain and fruitless mortification. It is God's great elevated rail system, sweeping over the heads of the struggling throngs who toil along the lower pavement when they might be borne along on His ascension pathway, by His own almighty impulse. It is God's great elevator, carrying us upward to the higher chambers of His palace without laborious effort on our part, even as others struggle up the winding stairs and faint by the way. It is God's great tidal wave bearing up the stranded ship until she floats above the bar without straining engines or struggling seamen. It is God's great law of evaporation lifting up by the warm sunbeams the mighty iceberg which a thousand men could not raise a single inch. How easy all this! How mighty! How simple! How divine!

Have you come into the divine way of holiness? If so, how your heart must swell with gratitude as it echoes the truths of the words you have just read! If not, do you not long for it and will you not now unite in the prayer of our text, so that the very God of peace will sanctify you wholly?

## The nature of sanctification

What does this term "sanctify" mean? Is there any

better way of ascertaining it than by tracing its scriptural usage? We find it employed in three distinct and most impressive senses in the Old Testament.

It means to separate. This idea can be traced all through its use in connection with the ceremonial ordinances. The idea of separation is first suggested in the account of creation in Genesis. There, we see the essential figure of sanctification. God's first work in bringing order, law and light out of chaos was to separate, to put an expanse or gulf between the two worlds of darkness and light, of earth and heaven. He did not annihilate the darkness, but He separated it from the light. He also separated the land from the water and the waters of the sea from the vapors of the sky.

Subsequently, we see Him in the spiritual realm, separating His people. He separated the family of Seth from the worldly race of Cain. He separated Noah and his family from the ungodly world. He separated Abraham and his seed from an idolatrous family. He separated Israel from Egypt and the surrounding nations. The very meaning of the word church is "called out," or "separated." To each individual the same call still comes: "Separate yourselves"—"Come out from among them and be ye separate, saith the Lord, and touch not the unclean thing: and I will receive you, And will be a Father unto you, and ye shall be my sons and daughters" (2 Corinthians 6:17–18). "Having therefore these promises, dearly beloved, let us cleanse ourselves from all filthiness of the flesh and spirit, perfecting holiness in the fear of God" (2 Corinthians 7:1).

Sanctification then means our voluntary separation from evil. It is not the extinction of evil, it is the putting off, the laying aside of evil, the detaching of ourselves from it and placing an impassable gulf between. We are to separate ourselves not only from our past sins but from our sin, as a principle of life. We are not to try to improve and gradually ameliorate our unholy condition, but we are to put off the old life, to act as if it were no longer a part of us. We are to separate ourselves from our sinful self. We are to reckon ourselves dead indeed unto sin just as though we were no longer the same people.

**We are to say no**

With respect to every manifestation of evil, whether from within or from without, we are to refuse every suggestion and impulse not of God. We are to be in the attitude of negation and resistance, with our whole being saying no. We do not have to annihilate the evil or to resist it in our own strength. Rather, by a definite act of will, we are to separate ourselves from it, to hand it over to God and renounce it utterly, to give Him the absolute right to deal with it and destroy it. When we do so, God always follows our committal with His almighty power. He puts between us and the evil we renounce a gulf as deep as the bottomless grave of Christ and a wall as high as the foundations of the New Jerusalem. We separate ourselves, and God makes the separation good. This is the first decisive step in sanctification. It is an act of the will by which we renounce evil in every form, whether in its manifestations or in the sinful nature from which each separate act has sprung.

We also separate ourselves from the world and its embodiment of the old natural condition of things and the kingdom of the prince of evil. We recognize ourselves as not of the world even as Jesus was not of the world. We put off, not only that which is sinful, but that which is natural and human, so that it may die on the cross of Jesus and rise into a supernatural and divine life. "If any man be in Christ, he is a new creature: old things are passed away; behold all things are become new" (2 Corinthians 5:17).

The Holy Spirit leads us to a deeper separation, not only from the evil but from the earthly, lifting us into a supernatural life. He prepares us, even here, for that great transformation in which this corruptible shall put on incorruption and this mortal, immortality. Even so, Adam, who was of the earth, earthy even before he fell, shall give place to the second Man who was made a living spirit and who has lifted us up into His own likeness.

What, then, is the practical force of this thought? It is simply this. As God shows us our old sinful self and every evil working of our fallen nature, we are to hand those things over to Him, with the full consent of our will. We are to let Him separate us from those things and deliver us completely from their power. Then we are to reckon those things as no longer having control over us. And as He leads us further on to see things that might not be called sinful and yet that are not incorporated into His life and will, from these, also, we are to separate ourselves, surrendering them to Him. We are to let Him put to death all that is apart from Himself and raise us up in new, resurrection life.

We then see that we are delivered from the death struggle with evil and the irrepressible conflict with self. It is our part to simply hand over Agag for execution and gladly consent that the Lord should slay him utterly, blotting out the remembrance of Amalek forever. Have we thus separated ourselves? Ours must be the surrender. God will not put His hand on the evil until we authorize Him with our glad consent. Like Joab's army of old, He encamps before our city and sends us the message that Sheba must die or the city perish. But our own hands must deliver Sheba over.

Have you done so? Will you even now with glad consent lay your hand upon the blessed Sin-offering's head and transfer your sinful heart and the dearest idol it has known to Him "who was made sin for us who knew no sin that we might be made the righteousness of God in him"?

## Sanctification means dedication

Sanctification also means dedication. Sanctification is not only a separation *from* but a separation *to*. The radical idea of the word is to set apart to be the property of another. The complement of this act, which we have already partly described, is this positive side in which we offer ourselves to God for His absolute ownership. We let Him possess us as His peculiar property, preparing us for His purpose and working out in us all His holy and perfect will. This is the meaning of the appeal made by Paul to the Romans: "I beseech you therefore, brethren, by the mercies of God, that ye present your bodies a living sacrifice, holy, acceptable to God, which is your reasonable service." This is the meaning of the phrase "God's peculiar people." Literally it means a people for a possession. The Scriptures can appeal to us to walk in holiness, because we are not our own. We are bought with a price, and we should glorify God in our bodies which belong to God.

It is true that God has bought us, but His infinite

condescension refuses to compel our surrender. He will accept nothing but a voluntary gift. So, gladly constrained by His love, we feel privileged to belong to Him, to have Him stoop to take us in our worthlessness and to be responsible for all the risks of our moment-by-moment existence.

This is what the term consecration properly means. It is the voluntary surrender or self-offering of the heart, by the constraint of love, to be the Lord's. Its glad expression is, "I am my Beloved's." It must spring, of course, from faith. There must be the full confidence that we are safe in this abandonment. We are not falling over a precipice or surrendering ourselves to the hands of a judge. Rather, we are sinking into a Father's arms and stepping into an infinite inheritance. It is an infinite privilege to be permitted thus to give ourselves up to One who pledges Himself to make us all that we would love to be, all that His infinite wisdom, power and love will delight to accomplish in us. It is the clay yielding itself to the potter's hands that it may be shaped into a vessel unto honor, meet for the Master's use. It is the poor street waif consenting to become the child of a prince so that he may be cared for and educated, so that he may be prepared to inherit all the wealth of his benefactor. How ashamed we may well feel that we ever hesitated to make such a surrender or that we ever qualified it with any condition but His good and perfect will! Have you made this full surrender? If so, how gladly your whole being says "Amen" to all that has been said about the blessedness of being only the Lord's! If not, do it this moment! At His feet of love, prostrate yourself as a whole burnt offering and cry,

*Take my poor life and let it be,*
*Forever closed to all but Thee;*
*Seal Thou my heart, and let me wear*
*Thy pledge of love forever there.*

## Sanctification means to fill

Finally, sanctification means filling. The literal translation of the old Hebrew word to consecrate is "to fill the hand." It suggests the deepest truth in connection with sanctification. Christ Himself must be the substance and supply of our new spiritual life; He fills us with His own Spirit and holiness. After the most sincere consecration, we are but an empty possibility which He must make real. Even our consecration itself must look to Him for grace to make it faultless and acceptable. By His continual grace, our will must be purified and kept single and supremely fixed on Him. Our purity must be the imparting of His life; our peace, His peace within us. Our love must be the love of God shed abroad in our hearts. Our very faith, which receives all His grace, must be continually supplied from His own Spirit. We bring to Him but an empty hand, clean and open, and He fills it. We are but a capacity and He is the supply. We give ourselves to Him fully, understanding that we do not pledge the strength or goodness required to meet our consecration. We take Him for all. And He takes us, fully recognizing the responsibility which He assumes to make us all that He requires and keep us in His perfect will. What an exquisite rest this gives to the trusting heart! What an infinite grace on His part to meet us on such terms and bear for us so vast a responsibility!

## What God wants

Each of us has a splendid site for a heavenly temple. It looks out upon eternity and commands a view of all that is glorious in the possibilities of existence. But the house that is built upon it now is a worthless wreck. It is past improving. Our patching and repairing is worse than waste. What God wants of us is simply for us to give Him the possibilities of our lives and to let Him build upon them His own structure. He will construct temples of holiness that He will make His own abode. From the very foundations, the work must be new and divine. Jesus is the Author and Finisher of our faith, and the true attitude of the consecrated person is one of constantly yielding and constantly receiving.

This last view of sanctification gives boundless scope to our spiritual progress. It is here that the gradual phase of sanctification comes in. Commencing with a complete separation from evil and a complete dedication to God, sanctification now advances into all the fullness of Christ. It grows up to the measure of the stature of perfect personhood in Him, until every part of our beings is filled with God and becomes a channel to receive, a medium to reflect His grace and glory.

Have we learned this blessed significance of sanctification? Have we taken God Himself as the fullness of our emptiness and fountain of our spiritual life? Then, indeed we have entered upon an everlasting expansion and ascension. Forevermore these blessed words will deepen and broaden in their boundless meaning:

*Thou of life the Fountain art,*
  *Ever let me take of Thee;*
*Spring Thou up within my heart,*
  *Rise to all eternity.*

# What the Bible Says about Healing

*"What the Bible Says about Healing" (originally titled "The Scriptural Foundation," from* The Gospel of Healing*) proclaims Christ's interest in bringing the believer physical as well as spiritual healing. Simpson published this chapter as an article in* The Word, The Work and The World *in 1883, not long after he was remarkably healed of chronic illness. According to his own testimony, the faith to receive healing came as he carefully studied what the Bible had to say about physical healing. Simpson did not see healing as a modern innovation, but as a recovery of biblical truth long neglected by traditional theology. Drawing from both the Old and New Testaments, he shows divine healing to be the fruit of Christ's redemptive work and a blessing available to believers today.*

MAN HAS A TWOFOLD nature. He is both a material and a spiritual being. And both natures have been equally affected by the Fall. His body is exposed to disease; his soul is corrupted by sin. How blessed, therefore, to find that the complete scheme of redemption includes both natures. It provides for the restoration of physical as well as the renovation of spiritual life!

The Redeemer appears among men with His hands stretched out to our misery and need, offering both salvation and healing. He offers Himself to us as a Savior to the uttermost; His indwelling Spirit the life of our spirit; His resurrection body the life of our mortal flesh.

Jesus begins His ministry by healing all who have need of healing; He closes it by making full atonement for our sin on the cross. Then on the other side of the open tomb He passes into heaven, leaving the double commission for "all nations" and "alway, even unto the end of the world" (Matthew 28:19–20).

He says, "Go ye into all the world, and preach the gospel to every creature. He that believeth and is baptized shall be saved, but he that believeth not shall be damned. And these signs shall follow them that believe; In my name shall they cast out devils; . . . they shall lay hands on the sick, and they shall recover" (Mark 16:15–18).

This was "the faith . . . once delivered unto the saints" (Jude 3). What has become of it? Why is it not still universally taught and realized? Did it disappear with the apostolic age? Was it withdrawn when Peter, Paul and John were removed? By no means! It remained in the church for centuries and only disappeared gradually in the church's growing worldliness, corruption, formalism and unbelief.

With a reviving faith, with a deepening spiritual life, with a more marked and scriptural recognition of the Holy Spirit and the living Christ and with the nearer approach of the returning Master Himself, this blessed gospel of physical redemption is beginning to be restored to its ancient place. The church is slowly learning to reclaim what she never should have lost. But along with this there is also manifested such a spirit of conservative unbelief and cold, traditional theological rationalism as to make it necessary that we should "earnestly contend for the faith which was once delivered unto the saints."

## Faith must rest on the Word

First, we must be sure of our scriptural foundations. Faith must always rest on the Divine Word. The most important element in the "prayer of faith" is a full and firm persuasion that the healing of disease by simple faith in God is a part of the gospel and a doctrine of the Scriptures.

The earliest promise of healing is in Exodus 15:25–26: "There he made for them a statute and an ordinance, and there he proved them, and said, If thou wilt diligently hearken to the voice of the Lord thy God, and wilt do that which is right in his sight, and wilt give ear to his commandments, and keep all his statutes, I will put none of these diseases upon thee, which I have brought upon the Egyptians: for I am the Lord that healeth thee."

The place of this promise is most marked. It is at the very outset of Israel's journey from Egypt, like Christ's healing of disease at the opening of His ministry.

It comes immediately after Israel passed through the Red Sea. This event is distinctly typical of our redemption, and the journey of the Israelites in the wilderness is typical of our pilgrimage: "These things happened unto them for ensamples: and they are written for our admonition, upon whom the ends of the world are come" (1 Corinthians 10:11).

This promise, therefore, becomes ours as the redeemed people of God. And God meets us at the very threshold of our pilgrimage with the covenant of healing. He declares that, as we walk in holy and loving obedience, we shall be kept from sickness, which belongs to the old life of bondage we have left behind us forever.

Sickness belongs to the Egyptians, not to the people of God. And only as we return spiritually to Egypt do we return to its malarias and perils. This is not only a promise; it is "a statute and an ordinance." And so, corresponding to this ancient statute, the Lord Jesus has left for us in James 5:14 a distinct ordinance of healing in His name, as sacred and binding as any of the ordinances of the gospel.

In Psalm 105:37 we read of the actual fulfillment of that promise: "He brought them forth also with silver and gold: and there was not one feeble person among their tribes." Although they did not fulfill their part in the covenant, God kept His word. And so, although our faith and obedience are often defective, if Christ is our surety and if our faith will claim His merits and His name, we too shall see the promise fulfilled.

**Satan the source**

The story of Job is one of the oldest records of history. It gives us a view of the source from which sickness came—in this case, Satan (Job 1–2). It also reveals the course of action that brings healing—that is, taking the place of humble self-judgment at the mercy seat. If ever a sickroom was unveiled, it was that of the man of Uz. But we see no physician there, no human remedy, only a looking unto God as his Avenger. And when Job renounces his self-righteousness and self-vindication and takes the place where God is seeking to bring him—that of self-renunciation and humility—he is healed.

The psalms of David are a record of many afflictions. But God is always the deliverer, and God alone: "Bless the Lord, O my soul, and forget not all his benefits: who forgiveth all thine iniquities; who healeth all thy diseases" (Psalm 103:2–3). We see no human hand. The psalmist looks to heaven as directly for healing as he does for pardon, and in the same breath he cries: "Who forgiveth all thine iniquities; who healeth all thy diseases." It is a complete healing—*all* his diseases—as universal and lasting as the forgiveness of his sins. And how glorious and entire that was is evident enough: "As far as the east is from the west, so far hath he removed our transgressions from us" (103:12). But here, as in the case of Job, there is an intimate connection between sickness and sin, and both must be healed together.

Asa was a king who had begun his reign by an act of simple, implicit trust in God when human resources utterly failed him. By that trust he won one of the most glorious victories of history (2 Chronicles 14:9–12). But success corrupted him. It taught him to value too highly the arm of flesh. In his next great crisis Asa formed an alliance with Syria and lost the help of God (16:7–8). He refused to take warning from the prophet and rushed on to the climax of his earthly confidence.

Asa became sick. Here was a greater foe than the Ethiopians, but again he turned to man: "And Asa in the thirty and ninth year of his reign was diseased in his feet, until his disease was exceeding great: yet in his disease he sought not to the Lord, but to the physicians" (16:12). The outcome could not be more sad or sarcastic: "And Asa slept with his fathers" (16:13).

## The Old Testament evangel

It was Isaiah who delivered the great evangelical vision, the gospel in the Old Testament, the very mirror of the coming Redeemer. And at the front of his prophetic message, prefaced by a great Amen—the only "surely" in the chapter—is the promise of healing: "Surely he hath borne our griefs, and carried our sorrows . . . and with his stripes we are healed" (Isaiah 53:4–5). It is the strongest possible statement of complete redemption from pain and sickness by Christ's life and death. And these are the very words Matthew quotes afterward, under the inspired guidance of the Holy Spirit (Matthew 8:17), as the explanation of Jesus' universal works of healing.

Our English version of Isaiah does only imperfect justice to the force of the original. The translation in Matthew is much better: "Himself took our infirmities, and bare our sicknesses." A literal translation of Isaiah would be: "Surely he hath borne away our sicknesses and carried away our pains."

Any person who will refer to such a familiar commentary as that of Albert Barnes on Isaiah, or to any other Hebrew authority, will see that the two words denote respectively *sickness* and *pain*. And the words for "bear" and "carry" denote not mere sympathy but actual substitution and the utter removal of the thing borne.

Therefore, as Jesus Christ has borne our sins, He

has also borne away and carried off our sicknesses, yes, and even our pains. Abiding in Him, we may be fully delivered from both sickness and pain. Thus "by his stripes we are healed." Blessed and glorious gospel! Blessed and glorious Burden-Bearer!

And so the ancient prophet beholds in vision the Redeemer coming first as a great Physician and then hanging on the cross as a great Sacrifice. The evangelists have also described Him so. For three years He was the great Healer, and then for six hours of shame and agony He was the dying Lamb.

### Jesus fulfills prophecy

Matthew, inspired by God, quotes Isaiah 53:4–5 as the reason why Jesus healed all who were sick: "He . . . healed all that were sick: that it might be fulfilled which was spoken by Esaias the prophet, saying, Himself took our infirmities, and bare our sicknesses" (Matthew 8:16–17).

It was not that Jesus might give His enemies a vindication of His Deity, but that He might fulfill the character presented of Him in ancient prophecy. Had He not done so, He would not have been true to His own character. If He did not still do so, He would not be "Jesus Christ the same yesterday, and to day, and for ever" (Hebrews 13:8). These healings were not occasional but continual, not exceptional but universal. Jesus never turned any away. "He . . . healed all that were sick." "As many as touched him were made whole." He is still the same.

This was the work of Jesus' life, and God would not have us forget that His Son spent more than three years in deeds of power and love before He went up to Calvary to die. We need that living Christ quite as much as we need Christ crucified. The Levitical types included the meal offering as much as the sin offering. And suffering humanity needs to feed upon the great loving Heart of Galilee and Bethany as much as on the Lamb of Calvary.

It would take entirely too long to examine in detail the countless records of Jesus' healing power and grace. He cured the leper, the lame, the blind, the paralytic, the impotent, the fever-stricken — all who "had need of healing." He linked sickness often with sin and forgave before He spoke the restoring word. He required their own personal touch of appropriating faith and bade them take the healing by rising up and carrying their beds.

His healing went far beyond His own immediate presence to reach and save the centurion's servant and the nobleman's son. How often He reproved the least question of His willingness to help and threw the responsibility of man's suffering on his own unbelief.

These and many more such lessons crowd every page of the Master's life and reveal to us the secret of claiming His healing power. What right has anyone to explain these miracles as mere types of spiritual healing and not as specimens of what He still is ready to do for all who trust Him? Such was Jesus of Nazareth.

## Jesus empowers others to heal

But was this blessed power to die with Jesus at Calvary? Jesus does not so indicate. "Verily, verily, I say unto you, He that believeth on me, the works that I do shall he do also; and greater works than these shall he do; because I go unto my Father" (John 14:12). Jesus makes it emphatic — "verily, verily" — as if He knew it was something mankind was sure to doubt. It is no use to tell us that this meant that the church after Pentecost was to have greater spiritual power and do greater spiritual works by the Holy Spirit than Jesus Himself did, inasmuch as the conversion of the soul is a greater work than the healing of the body. Jesus says, "The works that I do shall he do also," as well as the "greater works than these." That is, Jesus' followers are to do the same works that He Himself did and greater also.

Even during His life on earth Jesus sent out the 12 apostles. Then He sent out the 70 as forerunners of the whole host of the Christian eldership (for the 70 were in effect the first elders of the Christian age, corresponding to the 70 elders of Moses' time) with full power to heal. And when Jesus was about to leave the world, He left on record both these commissions in the most unmistakable terms.

## A twofold commission

"Go ye into all the world, and preach the gospel to every creature. He that believeth and is baptized shall be saved; but he that believeth not shall be damned. And these signs shall follow them that believe; In my name they shall cast out devils; they shall speak with new tongues; they shall take up serpents; and if they drink any deadly thing, it shall not hurt them; they shall lay hands on the sick, and they shall recover" (Mark 16:15–18).

Here is the commission of the twofold gospel given to them and the assurance of Christ's presence and unchanging power. What right have we to preach one part of the gospel without the other? What right have we to hold back any of God's grace from a perishing world? What right have we to go to unbelievers and

demand their acceptance of our salvation message
without these signs following? What right have we to
explain their absence from our ministry by trying to
eliminate them from God's Word or to consign them
to an obsolete past?

Christ promised the signs, and they followed as
long as Christians continued to believe and expect
them. It is important to observe Young's translation of
verse 17: "Signs shall follow them that believe these
things." The signs shall correspond to the extent of
their faith.

By such mighty "signs and wonders" the church
was established in Jerusalem, Samaria and unto the
uttermost parts of the earth. The unbelief of the world
needs these signs today as much as in the apostolic
times. During the apostolic age these manifestations
of healing power were by no means confined to the
apostles. Philip and Stephen were as gloriously used
as Peter and John.

In First Corinthians 12:9–30, "the gifts of healings"
are spoken of as widely diffused and universally
understood among the endowments of the church.
But the apostolic age was soon to close; were the gifts
to be continued, and if so, by whom? By what limitation was the church to be preserved from fanaticism
and presumption? By what commission was healing
to be perpetuated to the end of time and placed within
the reach of all God's suffering saints?

The answer is in James 5:14, to which we turn again
with deep interest: "Is any sick among you? let him
call for the elders of the church; and let them pray
over him, anointing him with oil in the name of the
Lord: and the prayer of faith shall save the sick, and

the Lord shall raise him up; and if he have committed sins, they shall be forgiven him."

Notice first who gives this commission. It is James—James, who had authority to say, in summing up the decrees of the council at Jerusalem, "My sentence is. . . ." He is the man who is named first by Paul himself among the pillars of the church (see Galatians 2:9).

Observe to whom this power is committed. Not to the apostles, who are now passing away; not to men and women of rare gifts or difficult to contact. It was given to the elders—the men most likely to be within reach of every sufferer, the men who are to continue till the end of the age.

Notice the time at which this commission is given. It was not at the beginning, but at the close of the apostolic age. It was not for that generation, but for the one that was just rising and all the succeeding ages. Indeed, these New Testament letters were not widely circulated in their own time, but were mainly designed "for our admonition, upon whom the ends of the world are come."

Again, observe the nature of the ordinance enjoined. It is "the prayer of faith" and the "anointing . . . with oil in the name of the Lord." This was not a medical anointing, for it was not to be applied by a physician, but by an elder. It must, naturally, be the same anointing we read of in connection with the healing of disease by the apostles (for instance, Mark 6:13).

Any other interpretation would be strained and contrary to the obvious meaning of the custom as our Lord and His apostles observed it. In the absence of any explanation to the contrary, we are bound to believe that it was the same—a symbolic religious ordinance expressive of the power of the Holy Spirit, whose peculiar emblem is oil.

The Greek Orthodox church still retains the ordinance, but the Roman Catholic church has changed it into a mournful preparation for death. It is a beautiful symbol of the Divine Spirit of life taking possession of the human body and breathing into it God's vital energy.

## Divine healing is a command

Divine healing ceases to be a mere privilege. It is the Divine prescription for disease, and no obedient Christian can safely ignore it. Any other method of dealing with sickness is unauthorized. This is God's plan. This makes faith simple and easy. We have only to obey in childlike confidence; God will fulfill.

Once more, we must not overlook the connection of sickness with sin. There is here the suggestion that the trial has been a Divine chastening and requires self-judgment, penitence and pardon. There is the blessed assurance that both pardon and healing may be claimed together in His name.

If more were needed than the testimony of James, then John, the last of the apostles and the one who best knew the Master's heart, has left a tender prayer: "Beloved, I wish [pray] above all things that thou mayest prosper and be in health, even as thy soul prospereth" (3 John 2). By this prayer we may know our Father's gentle concern for our health as well as for our souls. When God breathes such a prayer for us, we need not fear to claim it for ourselves. But as we do, we must not forget that our health will be even as our soul prospers.

In Ephesians 5:30 we note a union between our body and the risen body of the Lord Jesus Christ: "We are members of his body, of his flesh, and of his bones." We have the right to claim for our mortal frame the vital energy of Christ's perfect life. He has given His life for us, and it is all-sufficient.

"If the Spirit of him that raised up Jesus from the dead dwell in you, he that raised up Christ from the dead shall also quicken your mortal bodies by his Spirit that dwelleth in you" (Romans 8:11). This promise cannot refer to the future resurrection. That resurrection will be by the "voice of the Son of God" (John 5:25), not the Holy Spirit. This is a present dwelling in and a quickening by the Spirit. And it is a quickening of the "mortal body," not the soul.

What can this be but physical restoration? The physical restoration is the direct work of the Holy Spirit, and only they who know the indwelling of the Divine Spirit can receive it. It was the Spirit of God who wrought the miracles of Jesus Christ on earth (Matthew 12:28). And if we have the same Spirit dwelling in us, we shall experience the same works.

## Not simply healing but health

Paul expressed his physical experience this way: "Always bearing about in the body the dying of the Lord Jesus, that the life also of Jesus might be made manifest in our body. For we which live are alway delivered unto death for Jesus' sake, that the life also of Jesus might be made manifest in our mortal flesh" (2 Corinthians 4:10–11).

Paul knew constant peril, infirmity and physical suffering—probably by persecution and even violence. But it came in order that the healing, restoring and sustaining power and life of Jesus might be the more constantly manifest in his very body. And this for the encouragement of suffering saints—"for your sakes" (4:15). His life was a constant miracle that it might be to all persons a pledge and monument of the promise made to him for all who might thereafter suffer. This life, he tells us, was "renewed day by day" (4:16). The healing power of Christ is dependent on our continual abiding in Him and, like all God's gifts, is renewed day by day.

Christ did not say, "I *will be* with you alway." That would have suggested a break. He said, "I *am*"—an unchanging now, a presence never withdrawn, a love, a nearness, a power to heal and save as constant and as free as ever, even unto the end of the world. "Jesus Christ the same yesterday, and to day, and for ever."

Thus have we traced the teachings of the Holy Scriptures from Exodus to Patmos. We have seen God giving His people the ordinance of healing at the very outset of their pilgrimage. We have seen it illustrated in the ancient dispensation in the sufferings of Job, the songs of David and the sad death of Asa. We have seen Isaiah's prophetic vision of the coming Healer. We have seen the Son of man coming to fulfill that picture to the letter; we have heard Him tell His weeping disciples of His unchanging presence with them. We have seen Him transmit His healing power to their hands. And we have seen those followers hand down this gospel of healing to us and to the church of God until the latest ages of time.

What more evidence can we ask? What else can we do but believe, rejoice, receive and proclaim this great salvation to a sick and sinking world?

CHAPTER

6

# Paul and Divine Healing

*"Paul and Divine Healing" (from* The Lord for the
Body) *actually emphasizes divine health more than
divine healing. The apostle Paul said more about
Christ's provision for the body than any other New
Testament writer. Simpson shows from Paul's life and
teachings his firm faith in the Lord for the body as well
as for the soul and spirit. Paul trusted Christ for health
as well as healing. He saw Him as the source of physical
strength for the believer. The apostle's own physical trials
gave him every opportunity to test this doctrine and find
it true.*

*For me to live is Christ, and to die is gain. But if I live in the
flesh, this is the fruit of my labour: yet what I shall choose I
wot not. For I am in a strait betwixt two, having a desire to
depart, and to be with Christ; which is far better: Nevertheless to abide in the flesh is more needful for you. And having
this confidence, I know that I shall abide and continue with
you all for your furtherance and joy of faith (Philippians
1:21–25).*

THE APOSTLE PAUL was a pattern of our spiritual life in Christ. But he was also a striking example of our right and privilege to receive the life of our Lord Jesus Christ into our mortal frames. We may take Jesus for our physical strength as truly as for our spiritual needs.

Paul's life was a marvelous spiritual triumph in the face of unparalleled difficulties, pressures and sufferings. He seemed to live a charmed life; neither Jewish rods nor Roman dungeons nor hardships of any kind could hinder his singular service for Christ or shorten his triumphant course.

What was the secret of that marvelous physical life? The answer involves the whole doctrine of divine healing and reveals to us its deepest and highest principles.

## The standpoint of divine healing

It is good for us to approach every biblical truth from the right standpoint. Promises unreservedly true and meant for our enjoyment may be beyond our reach because we are not approaching them from the right direction or because we are not standing on the true ground of faith. In the verses already quoted, the apostle discloses the standpoint from which he was able to trust God for his body. It was because his life was not his own, but so dedicated to Jesus that he could truly say, "For me to live is Christ." It was because he had been delivered from the fear of death so fully that he could honestly say, "For me to die is gain." Paul did not want to live for his own sake, but for the sake of his Master only and for the sake of others. Therefore he could say in confidence, "I know that I shall abide and continue with you all."

Paul had completely renounced his own will in the matter of life or death. He claimed divine health not because it was his will, but because it was his Master's will and for his Master's glory. This is sublimely expressed in his noble words to the elders of Ephesus: "Neither count I my life dear unto myself, so that I might finish my course with joy, and the ministry, which I have received of the Lord Jesus, to testify the gospel of the grace of God" (Acts 20:24). Paul counted his life dear, but not for himself. He would have preferred to be with his blessed Master. But he counted his life dear because the Lord and the Lord's people needed him. Life was a sacred trust. Therefore, he could take it from his Master without a doubt or fear and go forward into the perils and privations that he knew awaited him.

This is the standpoint of divine healing. This is the ground of faith. This is the only place where we have a right to claim any of God's promises. So long as we want blessings for ourselves, they are selfish blessings. We must relinquish our rights and claims and take everything only for Christ. Then we can claim God's promises, because it is for God we are claiming them, and it is God's interest more than ours to bless us.

This was aptly expressed by a dear old saint who used to say when he got into any trouble, "Your property is in danger! Lord, take care of Your property!" He was so wholly the Lord's that he could honestly feel that in looking after himself he was looking after the Lord's property.

When we are Christ's, all things are ours. May God bring us to the point where we let go of life itself, as a personal desire, and then take it back as God's will and

God's choice and for His service and glory. It is the old story of Mount Moriah. It is Isaac laid down and then given back as God's Isaac and no longer as ours. We gain by losing, we lose by holding. The surrendered life is the only safe life. Letting go is twice possessing.

## The secret of divine healing

Paul had a secret. It was a very definite secret and expressed the philosophy of his physical life. It was exactly the same secret that he had for his spiritual life—"Not I but Christ liveth in me."

Paul had no sanctification of his own, but it was all summed up in the indwelling life of Christ. And so Paul claimed no physical strength of his own, but he had learned the secret of resting in the physical life of his Master. He had learned to live on the supernatural vitality he received from Christ, "renewed day by day."

Listen to him as he says, "Always bearing about in the body the dying of the Lord Jesus, that the life also of Jesus might be made manifest in our body. For we which live are alway delivered unto death for Jesus' sake, that the life also of Jesus might be made manifest in our mortal flesh" (2 Corinthians 4:10–11).

We find a little expression here repeated twice: "the life also of Jesus." Paul had two lives. He had his own life which was frail and mortal and always ready to die. But he had another life, "the life also of Jesus." When his own physical strength gave way, then the life of Jesus came to his aid and carried him through. In other words, he had residing in him the very Person of his blessed Master, and Christ's supernatural life sustained his vital energy. When he was ready to sink exhausted and all his powers had failed, there came to him directly from Christ through the Holy Spirit a quickening that revived and restored him. God was sufficient for all his needs.

Now, we may not understand this. We cannot understand it unless we know the secret, too. It is like a coded message. We must know the code to make any meaning of it. And the key to this experience is the personal knowledge of the Lord Jesus Christ in our own beings.

We find it confirmed by the whole story of Paul's life. For example, after Paul had preached the gospel, with wonderful power, to a heathen audience at Lystra, the jealous Jews from Iconium and Antioch came and set the people against him. They incited a cruel riot and persuaded the mob to attack Paul. The rioters dragged Paul through the streets of the city and stoned him, leaving him for dead. (We may be quite sure these enemies of Paul, when they had a chance to kill him, did not stop halfway.) As far as they could see, Paul was dead. But it was just then that "the life of Jesus" asserted itself. And so we read, simply but with sublime eloquence, "Howbeit, as the disciples stood round about him, he rose up, and came into the city, and the next day he departed with Barnabas to Derbe. And when they had preached the gospel to that city, and had taught many, they returned again to Lystra, and to Iconium, and Antioch" (Acts 14:20–21).

There we see the power of Christ revealed in the hour of utter despair. As his brethren stood around him in concerned prayer, the Holy Spirit aroused his sinking life. Jesus touched him with His own life, and lo! that life of Christ quickened his mortal flesh. Paul sprang to his feet and went on to his work. The next day we find him, not in a hospital, or on a long vacation, but preaching the gospel, returning to the very place where he had been maltreated and almost killed. He went about his work quietly, triumphantly, taking his healing for granted as though it were just the thing to be expected.

So again, we find Paul at another point in his life, telling the Corinthians of the trouble that came to him and Timothy in Asia: "We were pressed out of measure, above strength, insomuch that we despaired even of life: But we had the sentence of death in ourselves, that we should not trust in ourselves, but in God which raiseth the dead: Who delivered us from so great a death, and doth deliver: in whom we trust, that he will yet deliver us" (2 Corinthians 1:8–10).

Here is a very clear experience of divine healing. The apostle was sick unto death. He despaired of life. When he looked at himself, the only answer seemed to be death. Paul was not equal to it. He was pressed above measure and above strength. Yet there was another life, the life of his risen Lord, the strength of "God which raiseth the dead," on which he depended. And from his own sinking life he looked up to the endless life of Jesus and claimed it in all its resurrection power. In triumph he could shout, "Who delivered . . . doth deliver . . . he will yet deliver."

This is the secret of divine healing. It is union with One who is our physical Head as well as the source of our spiritual life. It is to be in touch with the Son of man who arose from the dead in the power of an endless life. He is the Head of our body. He has taught us to understand that "we are members of his body, of his flesh, and of his bones" (Ephesians 5:30). In another place the apostle tells us that our "bodies are the members of Christ" (1 Corinthians 6:15). The Lord is for the body, and the body is for the Lord. Why should we not understand and claim Paul's secret too?

This divine health does not mean immortality—life that never can die. It does mean participation in the life of our risen Lord in a measure that makes us equal to every duty, every labor and every pressure until our life work ceases and the Master either calls us to Himself or comes to meet us. Have you learned the secret: "the life also of Jesus"?

## The practical working of Paul's secret

Paul did not presume on his own constitutional strength. On the contrary, he knew his weakness and personal insufficiency. There is every reason to believe that Paul was naturally feeble rather than robust. His constant exposures, hardships and sufferings had reduced him many times to the very verge of prostration and even death. He spoke of the infirmity of his flesh. "For we which live are alway delivered unto death for Jesus' sake" (2 Corinthians 4:11). "Always bearing about in the body the dying of the Lord Jesus" (v. 10). But his own weakness did not hinder his taking the strength of the Lord Jesus and being enabled thereby for all that the Master required of him.

Paul's health and strength were a divine paradox. "When I am weak, then am I strong," he could most truly say. In himself he was physically weak. But in reliance upon the physical strength of an indwelling Lord, he was stronger than himself. He was better equipped for his work than even perfect health could have made him.

Here lies the deep secret of divine healing and the explanation of Paul's singular experience recorded in

Second Corinthians 12. The "thorn in the flesh" — whatever that thorn was — was not removed, but more strength was given him than if it had been removed. If the "thorn" was a spiritual trial, the trial was not removed, but extra grace was added. If it was a physical weakness, it was not withdrawn, but extra strength was supplied. So Paul was actually stronger than if he had been delivered from the particular trouble.

He could say, "I take pleasure in infirmities, . . . for Christ's sake: . . . that the power of Christ may rest upon me" (2 Corinthians 12:9, 11). Paul's health was divine strength given in human weakness: "Though the outward man perish," (the natural and physical constitution may seem to decay) "yet the inward man" — the divine life, by Christ's strength — "is renewed day by day" (2 Corinthians 4:16).

Paul's experience of divine health was compatible with the greatest pressures, the severest hardships, the most perilous exposures and the most uncongenial and unfavorable surroundings. Some of his life was spent in damp, unhealthy dungeons. He was exposed to inclement weather, the lack of food and sleep. A night and a day he was adrift at sea. He was shipwrecked, he was beaten, he was pelted with stones. Not usually does the human frame sustain such unspeakable pressures. And yet through them all he marched triumphantly, always ready for whatever service the Master had for him. "We are troubled on every side," he could say, "yet not distressed; we are perplexed, but not in despair; persecuted, but not forsaken; cast down, but not destroyed" (2 Corinthians 4:8–9). The severest pressures only served to highlight the glory and strength of his Lord. "We have this treasure in earthen vessels, that the excellency of the power may be of God, and not of us"(2 Corinthians 4:7).

Paul's physical strength was sustained by continual dependence on the Lord Jesus. He rested on Christ for his physical as well as his spiritual life. In speaking of his day-by-day renewal, he said, "we look not at the things which are seen, but at the things which are not seen" (2 Corinthians 4:18).

The renewing was "day by day" and only while he looked to the unseen sources of his strength. He did not receive one tremendous miracle which carried him through life. He had learned what Jesus had so clearly unfolded in regard to His own life, "As the living Father hath sent me, and I live by the Father: so he that eateth me, even he shall live by me" (John 6:57). Feeding upon Christ, he lived by Him. He could truly say in the language which he employed elsewhere and in another connection, "In him we live, and move, and have our being" (Acts 17:28).

Have we learned thus moment by moment to live upon Christ's life? As outward pressure increases and personal strength diminishes, have we taken a stronger hold upon Christ's everlasting strength? As we wait upon the Lord, we renew our strength until we shall "mount up with wings as eagles; . . . run, and not be weary; . . . walk, and not faint" (Isaiah 40:31). This was the physical life of Paul. This is the privilege of every believing and obedient child of God.

# The Coming of the King

*"The Coming of the King" (from* Christ in the Bible — Matthew) *proclaims the ultimate gospel of a returning Lord Jesus Christ. In the fall of 1903, Simpson initiated a series of sermons on the Gospel of Matthew that were subsequently published as part of his* Christ in the Bible *series. The study of Matthew 24 provides a sweeping overview of the church age and a panorama of events related to Christ's second coming. This treatment of Jesus' Olivet discourse is a good summary of Simpson's teaching on Bible prophecy. Simpson was more practical than speculative in matters of eschatology. The relationship of world missions and Christ's return was his overriding concern.*

*Watch, therefore, for ye know neither the day nor the hour wherein the Son of man cometh (Matthew 25:13).*

OUR LORD HAD ACCEPTED for the time the homage of the multitude and the titles and honors of the Son of David and the throne of the Messiah! If the nation had only heartily and truly received Him, we can scarcely dream of the results that might have followed. An eloquent writer has ventured to express something of such a dream, picturing the Lord Jesus completing His sacrifice, not through wicked enemies, but by His Father offering Him up even as Abraham offered Isaac on Mt. Moriah. This is followed by His glorious resurrection and His sitting down upon David's throne, fulfilling for Israel and the world the vision of ancient prophecy without the dark and dreadful centuries of Israel's rejection and punishment.

But this was not to be. Indeed, it could not be with all the other prophecies yet to be fulfilled. And so "He came unto his own, and his own received him not" (John 1:11). Israel as a nation rejected Him, and ages have to pass before He can come to them again as their King and fulfill to them the vision of the promised glory.

But He will surely come, and the next portion of Matthew's gospel unfolds to us in His own prophetic words the panorama of events that will lead up to that great Appearing.

The discourses related in Matthew 24 and 25 were delivered by our Lord on Tuesday afternoon immediately after His great conflict with the rulers and on His way from the temple to His temporary home in Bethany. The first part of the address was no doubt uttered as they departed from the temple, probably through the Golden Gate, and walked down into the valley of Kedron. The last portion was likely concluded as He sat on the slopes of Olivet, looking down once more over the city at His feet. The interpretation of the discourse will be rendered more clear if we bear in mind the questions of the disciples to which it was intended to be an answer.

## Questions of the disciples

The disciples pointed out to Him the splendid stones and building of the temple, and He told them, "There shall not be left here one stone upon another, that shall not be thrown down." Immediately they ask Him three questions: "When shall these things be?" "What shall be the sign of thy coming?" "[What shall be the sign] of the end of the world?" (Matthew 24:2–3).

The first part of His discourse would therefore naturally be a reply to their first question, "When shall these things be?" namely, the destruction of Jerusalem. The later portion of His discourse would naturally refer to their other two questions, "What shall be the sign of thy coming, and of the end of the world?" It should be kept in mind that the term "world" here employed is not the usual Greek word for the material world. That would be "kosmos"; it is the word "aion," which means "the age," the order of events and the plan of Providence. The correct translation, therefore, is "the end of the age," for the end of the age will not necessarily bring the end of the world.

We shall group the Lord's teachings concerning His coming under a number of clearly defined headings which are brought out with great distinction in His discourses.

## Christ's coming and Israel

The relation of His coming to Israel and the destruction of Jerusalem was the first thing that entered their minds and His. It was also prominent with Matthew, whose gospel was specifically for Israel. He brings to the front, in all the Master's teaching, the special references of His addresses to the "chosen people." From 24:4–28, with the single exception of verse 14, the entire passage seems to apply to Israel and the judgments and sufferings that were to come upon them because of their rejection of the Messiah.

There would appear, however, to be two sections in the passage: one referring to the earlier tribulations of Jerusalem under the Romans, and the other to her later trials at the end of the age. To the Master's view, it seemed like one long perspective for Israel, beginning and ending with a fearful tragedy. Between these two sections, there is thrown in a brief parenthesis in verse 14, which describes the Christian age and the gospel among the Gentiles. For Israel, however, the prospect is dark and lurid, reaching its climax in spiritual delusion and national calamity without precedent or parallel.

This is in exact accordance with the predictions of Daniel and Zechariah. Referring to the first destruction of Jerusalem, Daniel had said: "The people of the prince that shall come shall destroy the city and the sanctuary; and the end thereof shall be with a flood, and unto the end of the war desolations are determined" (Daniel 9:26). And referring to the later afflictions of Jerusalem at the end of the age, Daniel had said: "There shall be a time of trouble, such as never was since there was a nation, even to that same time" (Daniel 12:1).

Zechariah also had even more explicitly described these calamities, especially in the later days of Israel.

*It shall come to pass, that in all the land, saith the Lord, two parts therein shall be cut off and die; but the third part shall be left therein. Behold, the day of the Lord cometh, and thy spoil shall be divided in the midst of thee. For I will gather all nations against Jerusalem to battle; and the city shall be taken, and the houses rifled, and the women ravished; and half of the city shall go forth into captivity, and the residue of the people shall not be cut off from the city (Zechariah 13:8; 14:1–2).*

Our Lord's predictions are in exact accordance with these terrible forewarnings. No doubt much of this was fulfilled when the Romans captured the city under Titus and Vespasian, but much of it yet must be in store.

## The Christian age

His coming with reference to the Christian age is condensed into a single verse: "This gospel of the kingdom shall be preached in all the world for a witness unto all nations; and then shall the end come" (Matthew 24:14). This is all that the Master says about the Gentile parenthesis which we call the Christian age and which has now been running its course for 19 centuries. A single phrase of concentrated light and truth covers all this long period.

Let us not think, in our self-conceit, that we Gentiles monopolize the whole prophetic word. Writing to the Gentiles, the apostle Paul said: "I would not, brethren, that ye should be ignorant of this mystery, lest ye should be wise in your own conceits; that blindness in part is happened to Israel, until the fulness of the Gentiles be come in" (Romans 11:25). That is to say, we Gentiles have received the gospel for a time because Israel refused it, but after our time of opportunity is over, Israel's will return. This 14th verse described the Gentile age during which this gospel of the kingdom (and there is but one gospel) is to be "preached in all the world for a witness unto all nations." When this shall have been done to the full extent, our Lord assures us *the end will come.*

The evangelization of the world and its universal accomplishment is the most distinct landmark of the Lord's coming. Our Lord's prediction here is in exact accord with the words of the apostle Peter, "God at the first did visit the Gentiles, to take out of them a people for his name. . . . After this I will return, and will build again the tabernacle of David, which is fallen down" (Acts 15: 14–16). This is the age in which we are living. This is the time of grace for the Gentiles. Let us not allow "the time of our visitation" to pass by neglected; let us not fail as the disciples of Christ to meet our high and holy trust to send the gospel as a witness to all nations that we may hasten the coming of our Lord.

### The Great Tribulation

Coincident with Israel's latest trials will be that time of trouble known in prophecy as the Great Tribulation. Speaking of it our Lord says: "Then shall be great tribulation, such as was not since the beginning of the world to this time, no, nor ever shall be. And except those days should be shortened, there should be no flesh saved: but for the elect's sake those days shall be shortened" (Matthew 24:21–22).

This time of trouble will be brought about by a variety of conditions. One of them will be God's judgment upon this sinful world; another, the outbreak of satanic power and malignity. Still another

will be the power of Antichrist and his assaults upon
Israel and upon all divine institutions that shall remain
in the world. Yet another element will be the absence
of most of God's people, for the Church will have
been withdrawn at the beginning of the tribulation
and its watching and holy members caught up to meet
the Lord in the air.

A world without the godly, a world controlled by
Antichrist, a world under the personal government of
Satan and a world beneath the outpourings of God's
vials of wrath—surely, that is a picture dark enough
to make us watch and pray that "we may escape these
things which shall come to pass." It is the promise of
Christ to the faithful ones: "I also will keep thee from
the hour of temptation, which shall come upon all the
world, to try them that dwell upon the earth" (Revelation 3:10b).

### His public appearing

> *Immediately after the tribulation of those days shall the
> sun be darkened, and the moon shall not give her light,
> and the stars shall fall from heaven, and the powers of
> the heavens shall be shaken: And then shall appear the
> sign of the Son of man in heaven: and then shall all the
> tribes of the earth mourn, and they shall see the Son of
> man coming in the clouds of heaven with power and
> great glory (Matthew 24:29–39).*

This is the great Epiphany, the public appearance of
the Lord Jesus as distinguished from His Parousia or
His previous and secret coming for His own. Now,
however, after the tribulation He is to come in the
blaze of His glory openly and visibly before the eyes
of all the world, and as they see Him "all the tribes of

the earth shall mourn." It shall be a day of terror to this godless world, a day of destruction and judgment to the wicked nations that shall be found in opposition to His throne.

Notice the pronoun "they" instead of "ye." The Lord does not tell them that they are to see Him come; His disciples will be with Him when He comes. The world shall see Him, but we, His followers, will have no business there in that day of terror and dismay. God help us to be found ready and waiting so that we shall escape the tribulation and the day of wrath and be with Him above the storm.

> *I see that last and bloody sunset,*
> *I see the dread Avenger's form;*
> *I hear the Armageddon onset,*
> *But I shall be above the storm.*

### Caught up

Verses 40 and 41 form a separate picture, referring to the Parousia—His coming for His own. "As the days of Noah were, so shall also the coming of the Son of man be" (Matthew 24:37). Of this He is speaking when He says: "Then shall two be in the field; the one shall be taken, and the other left. Two women shall be grinding at the mill; the one shall be taken, and the other left" (24:40–41).

It is a little uncertain whether the passage in verse 31 also refers to this, "He shall send his angels with a great sound of a trumpet, and they shall gather together his elect from the four winds, from one end of heaven to the other." This may refer to the final gathering of the tribulation saints, still left on earth after the tribulation, at His public appearing. There is no doubt, however, that verses 40 and 41 must refer to the rapture of His saints. One by one they shall be caught up to meet Him in the air and the unready ones left behind. Are you ready for that Parousia, and will you be found in "that happy company?"

## Christ's coming is pre-millennial

The Lord introduces in the picture of His coming the remarkable natural similitude which He calls "the parable of the fig tree" (24:32). The peculiarity of the fig tree is that the fruit appears before the leaves, and the application of this to the Lord's coming is that the Lord Jesus will appear before the Millennium. It is not first the luxuriant foliage on the tree and then the fruit as a climax, but it is first the fruit and then the foliage. Or, to drop the figure, it is not first our cultural, social, scientific and religious progress and then Christ's coming to a world all ready to receive Him. On the contrary, it is first Christ Himself, and then, as the result of His coming, the revolution of modern society and the righting of all the world's ancient wrongs. The coming of Jesus Christ is not an evolution, but a revolution.

This is still further confirmed by the picture He gives us of the state of human society at His advent. Post-millenarians fondly describe the gradual progress of Christian influences and the improvement of the world. After a little while, they avow, things will be about right and we can expect the Lord to come down to congratulate us on the good work we have been able to do without Him.

The picture Jesus gives us is entirely different: "As the days of Noah were, so shall also the coming of the Son of man be." We know that the days of Noah were marked by wickedness and crime, and it would seem as if the two crimes most rampant in Noah's time, namely, violence and lust, are coming to the front again in our own day. While it is true that the elements of righteousness and spiritual power are making progress, and the good are better than they ever were before, there can be no doubt that the bad are worse, and the shadow grows as dark as the light grows bright.

## His coming is sudden

Verses 26, 42 and 44 of Matthew 24 tell us that the Lord's coming will be a shock to this complacent world. It will also be a surprise to the modern prophets who persist in knowing the very schedule of events and the times which the Father hath put in His own power.

It will not be a surprise to His waiting people. "But ye, brethren, are not in darkness, that that day should overtake you as a thief" (1 Thessalonians 5:4). They may not know the day or hour, but they shall know enough to be ready. But to the world it will be a startling, terrifying blow. "For when they shall say, peace and safety; then sudden destruction cometh upon them, as travail upon a woman with child; and they shall not escape" (1 Thessalonians 5:3). Even for us, the followers of Christ, the only safety is to be always ready.

## Christ's coming and judgment

Christ's first act at His coming will be to call His servants before Him in judgment. Then shall the faithful ministers receive a great reward. "Who then is a faithful and wise servant, whom his lord hath made ruler over his household, to give them meat in due season? Blessed is that servant, whom his lord when he cometh shall find so doing. Verily I say unto you, That he shall make him ruler over all his goods" (vv. 45–47).

This is the promise which speaks of the servants who shall be found true to His message and His flock. But, oh, how awful the doom of the false minister, of the man who has ignored the truth of the Lord's coming and in his heart has secretly hoped that it might not be. Encouraged by this false theology, he has yielded to ambition and self-aggrandizement and has been drawn into the spirit of controversy and worldliness. Alas for him!

> But and if that evil servant shall say in his heart, my lord delayeth his coming; and shall begin to smite his fellow servants, and to eat and drink with the drunken; the lord of that servant shall come in a day when he looketh not for him, and in an hour that he is not aware of, and shall cut him asunder, and appoint him his portion with the hypocrites: there shall be weeping and gnashing of teeth (24:48–51).

CHAPTER

8

# The Church in the Heavenlies

*"The Church in the Heavenlies" (from* The Highest
Christian Life) *declares our exalted position in Christ
Jesus and its practical aspects. The nature of the church
was a frequent theme in Simpson's preaching and writing. Particularly in his study of Ephesians, he addresses
the ministry of the church as revealed to Paul. Simpson
was at his best when explaining the types and figures of
speech used by biblical writers to express doctrinal truth.
His insights on the church as a building, a body and a
bride are rich in doctrinal content and applied truth. The
supreme object of the church, Simpson concludes, is the
reflection of the glory of Christ before the world.*

*Built upon the foundation of the apostles and prophets, Jesus
Christ himself being the chief corner stone; in whom all the
building fitly framed together groweth unto an holy temple in
the Lord (Ephesians 2:20–21).*
*There is one body, and one Spirit, even as ye are called in one
hope of your calling; . . . the whole body fitly joined together
and compacted by that which every joint supplieth, according
to the effectual working in the measure of every part, maketh*

*increase of the body unto the edifying of itself in love (Ephesians 4:4, 16).*

*For the husband is the head of the wife, even as Christ is the head of the church: . . . Christ also loved the church, and gave himself for it; that he might sanctify and cleanse it with the washing of water by the word, that he might present it to himself a glorious church, not having spot, or wrinkle, or any such thing; but that it should be holy and without blemish. . . . This is a great mystery: but I speak concerning Christ and the church (Ephesians 5:23, 25–27, 32).*

WE ARE ABOUT TO SEE THE CHURCH in the heavenlies. We are about to behold the blessings of the Spirit in the individual consummated in the collective body of the saints, the glorious church of the Lord Jesus Christ.

The parable of the treasure hid in the field, representing the people of God in their separate capacities, reaches its climax in the parable of the pearl of great price, where we behold God's people in their united capacity. That which is true of the disciples of Christ individually, is more completely and gloriously true of the whole company of disciples when they shall be gathered as one body under their living Head and glorious Lord.

This vision of the church, along with the kindred mystery of the indwelling of Christ in the individual heart, was given to Paul as one of the peculiar revelations of his ministry. "By revelation he made known unto me the mystery, . . ." he says, "which in other ages was not made known unto the sons of men, . . . that the Gentiles should be fellowheirs, and of the same body, and partakers of his promise in Christ by the gospel" (Ephesians 3:3, 5, 6).

Already in the theme of the preceding chapter, Paul has given us a hint of this great truth. Now, after speaking of the indwelling of Christ in the believer's heart and the marvelous revelation that it was fitted to bring of the unfathomable love of Christ, he adds "that ye might be able to comprehend with all saints the knowledge of the surpassing love of Christ."

Not singly can we grasp this mighty vision. It is only when we enter into the perfect fellowship of the body of Christ that we can know the fullness of our great salvation. If it is true in the natural world, "God never made an independent man, / 'Twould mar the general concord of His plan," much more is it true in the spiritual world. Here the whole progression of redemption is toward one grand consummation: the reconciling and uniting of all in one. God intends to crystallize in the church of Jesus Christ all His wisdom, power and love in creation and redemption. It will be a single ideal—the paragon of the universe, the glory of the ages to come, the bride of His own Son.

In Ephesians, the church is presented in three striking figures: the building, the body and the bride.

## The building

Architecture, one of the most attractive of the arts and sciences, has conceived and executed many wonderful buildings. Its crowning triumph is to embody in lifeless stone a living idea. This has been successfully accomplished in such creations as the Greek column, the Roman arch, the Byzantine porch, the Gothic spire, the Italian dome. Each conveys some distinct and impressive conception of grace, majesty or awe.

Gazing at the splendid dome of the capitol building

in Washington, D.C., the forest of pinnacles that rise from the marble towers of Milan Cathedral or the strange ethereal charm of that "Dream in Marble," the Taj Mahal at Agra, a person is conscious that mind has triumphed over matter, that stone is speaking unutterable thoughts and feelings to the cultivated mind. The supreme charm of the architect's design is unity. His conception is to produce a single building and a unique effect.

God is building a spiritual house on a similar principle, but it far transcends man's highest thought. He is rearing an invisible temple for the manifestation of His own infinite presence and glory. The only two structures ever built on earth by divine architecture are entirely controlled by this idea. They were expressive of the highest truths.

**The desert tabernacle**

Look at the tabernacle in the wilderness, the first church God ever built. Everything about it was eloquent of redemption and significant of Christ. The exterior, so plain and unattractive, and the interior, so glorious and resplendent, is an image of the church of Christ and her glorious Head and Lord, despised and rejected of men, yet "all glorious within." The court and the sacrificial altar and cleansing lavar proclaim the truths of salvation and sanctification. The Holy place and the golden lamps reveal not their own beauty, but the table of shewbread and the rich provision of that sacred chamber for the privileged worshipers. The air is laden with richest perfume, and the frankincense from the golden altar breathes throughout the chamber, speaking of the very presence of God—the breath of heaven and the wafted odors from the fields of God's paradise. Venture through the rent veil, and the winged cherubim, the blood-sprinkled mercy seat, the ark of the covenant and the awesome Shekinah speak of the innermost presence of God Himself and the highest truths of divine union and heavenly glory. The whole building was an object lesson of redemption and an exhibition of Jesus Christ.

The same was true of the temple that afterward rose on Mount Moriah on a grander scale, but with equal spiritual significance. Similarly, God intended His church to be an exhibition of His glorious gospel, His heavenly character and the riches of His grace. Its business here is to display Christ, to manifest God and to afford a channel for His revelation and indwelling among men. Its message to the world is, "The church of the living God [is] the pillar and ground (or support) of the truth" (1 Timothy 3:15b). "The tabernacle of God is with men, and he will dwell with them" (Revelation 21:3).

Whenever the Church becomes self-conscious and self-centered, she fails to accomplish her real divine calling. Her highest glory is to be seen only in the revealing of her Lord.

Deep and true is the lesson taught by the ancient legend of the three architects who brought to the oriental king their models for a temple of the sun. The first was of stone, finely chiseled and richly polished, and as the king beheld it he could only admire and praise the splendid work. The second was of gold, and well did the architect descant on the burnished walls as they reflected in every angle and facet the image of the sun itself. But the third presented a temple of glass so transparent that at first it was invisible.

It did not take long to show, as the sunlight poured unhindered through the transparent walls, that this was the true temple of the sun, reflecting not its own glory, but revealing and receiving in every part the glorious object to whose honor it was dedicated.

## Jesus is the cornerstone

This is the supreme object of the church of Jesus Christ, and only insofar as we are revealing and reflecting Him who is our Head are we accomplishing the object for which the church was founded.

Of this glorious building, Christ is the cornerstone. He is at once the foundation and the center. From that stone every vertical line is drawn. From that stone every horizontal line is projected. It unites the two walls, decides the true angle, and in relation to it every particle of the wall is located and erected.

As there is but one cornerstone, there is but one building. But if we look at the spiritual masonry of today we behold not so much a building as a block of buildings, scores of fragmentary structures, the foundations of human names and humanly constructed constitutions. Need we wonder that the walls are often off the plumbline and the square, that through the unguarded gates the money-changers have right of way, and that from within there often comes, not the Shekinah glory of the Master's presence, but the sad cry, "Behold, your house is left unto you desolate!" (Matthew 23:38).

## The church is one

The unity of the church is the point most strongly emphasized by the apostle in this passage. "There is one body and one spirit." There are not two ages of the church, the apostolic and the modern, but we are the same church which Christ founded and in which the apostles laid the first tier of masonry. We have the same promises, the same enduement of power and we should have the same manifestations of the presence and power of God.

Not only are we one chronologically, but we are one in diversity. Notwithstanding all the peculiarities of the individual character, the heart, the spirit, the life of the church is ever one. In the tabernacle there were hundreds of parts, but there was one building. There was no need that one should displace another. Each had its place. They were "fitly framed together," and placed in position they formed a unique and complete whole. So should the church of Jesus Christ be "fitly framed together," standing in the beauty of a unity the more perfect because of its diversity. Each of us is but a single part in the whole structure. If we shrink from our neighboring board or if we swell beyond our place so as to displace another, it is because we are not properly seasoned. We are not in the divine order and plan.

It is a great thing for every child of God to learn and fully understand what it means to be one of many; not *the* one, but only one. When we come to understand that God has millions of lives just as necessary and just as precious as ours, then we shall learn to give place to our brethren and keep rank in the host of God.

God's two ancient buildings, the Tabernacle and the Temple, were intended to set forth the two stages of the church's history — the earthly and the heavenly. That moving tabernacle represented the earthly church, with no continuing city and no inheritance below the skies. The glorious structure on Mount Moriah's height represented the heavenly Church, when all the materials shall have been gathered home and the universe shall come to gaze upon the jeweled walls of the New Jerusalem and behold the bride, the Lamb's wife.

## The body

The difference between a building and a body is immense. The building is mechancial; the body is organic. The first is put together by forces outside itself; the second grows from a force within itself. The building is a lifeless mass; the body is a living organism.

And so the apostle's thought advances to higher ground, for the church of Jesus Christ is not merely constructed, it is created. It is born. It is formed out of the very life of Christ, its living Head, and it grows in Him up to "the measure of the stature of the fulness of Christ." The science of anatomy is therefore much higher in the sphere of its investigations than that of architecture, and the study of the human body is fitted to afford a thousand illustrations of the beauty and significance of this striking figure. On these we cannot dwell in this brief space. It is enough that we individually realize the heart of the conception that in the body of Christ our life comes directly from Him. Our relationship with each other is dependent upon our relationship with the Head. Three points will suffice to bring out these truths.

1. We derive our life from the Head. As Eve was made out of Adam's substance, so the Church was born out of Christ. Every individual Christian is part of the life of his Lord. And as we sprang from Him, so

we must live by Him in intimate organic communion. His life is imparted to our threefold being — spirit, soul and body — and "in him we live, and move, and have our being." No one really belongs to the church of Christ who is not personally united to Christ in regeneration and communion.

2. He is the Head of authority and control. The head directs the members of the body, and so the church of Jesus Christ should be subject in everything to the will of her Lord. Instinctively every member should move obediently to the touch of the Head. By a thousand connecting chords of holy intuition, we may learn to catch the faintest intimation of His will and become responsive to His every thought and inspiration.

3. Our relationships to each other are in and through the Head, and only as we meet in Him can we be rightly adjusted to one another. The members of the body are related to each other only through the Head. Your fingers work together simply because they are both in direct contact with the brain. Let one be separated from its source of power, and it will at once be separated from its associate member.

A simple illustration will show how all true unity in the human body depends upon the brain. A person who both plays the organ and sings is using four members of his body in unison. His feet are pressing the pedals. His fingers are sweeping the keyboards and his eyes are watching the music score. His voice is in tune and time with notes of the book and the music of the organ. Here are four members acting in concert. How do they do so? Are the eyes to watch the finger? If so, how are they to watch the page? Is the voice to be thinking about the organ's keys? No. Each member is acting independently under direct orders from the brain. Through the one head they all produce the one melodious result.

Jesus is the secret of Christian harmony. If you and I come together with our separate thoughts and feelings, we shall never harmonize. We must suspend our personal lives and take Christ's life instead. "He is our peace," and in Him we can have unity and power. We should never touch people apart from Jesus. A heavenly halo of divine presence should ever encompass us, and, as we meet each other in this holy fellowship of divine life and love, we shall be one in Him. We shall fulfill the glorious ideal so finely described in Ephesians 4:15–16:

> But speaking the truth in love, may grow up into him in all things, which is the head, even Christ: From whom the whole body fitly joined together and compacted by that which every joint supplieth, according to the effectual working in the measure of every part, maketh increase of the body unto the edifying of itself in love.

## The bride

There is a still higher concept of the church. The building is a physical figure. The body is a physiological one. The Bridegroom and the bride take us into the deeper life of love. This is the figure which runs like a golden thread of divine romance through the whole story of revelation and redemption. It is as old as Eden. It reaches its consummation in the marriage of the Lamb.

How beautiful the picture that comes back to us from paradise! First, the bride was formed out of the body of Adam, and then she was given to Adam as his bride. So, too, the Church is born out of Christ and then wedded to Him.

In Ezekiel 16 there is a beautiful parable of this mystery of love. The prophet describes the foundling child lying in her blood, repulsive and utterly wretched. As the Lord passed by he saw her and had compassion on her. He washed her, robed her, educated her, trained her, crowned her with a halo of glory and then wedded her and made her all His own. So God has loved us, saved us, quickened us together with Him, and now He takes us into this intimate and unspeakable relationship which all earthly figures fail fully to express.

Let us ask the Holy Spirit to purify our minds from every shade of mere human passion or affection. Just as a breath of warm, moist air can cloud the face of a mirror, so the courseness of earthly passion can obscure this exquisite figure God wants us to see. This divine relationship is as holy as the Shekinah light. Flesh and blood cannot inherit this kingdom of heaven. Only the death-born life can enter here. This union with Christ meets our entire being and satisfies our whole nature. It thrills with holy joy the heart of love and quickens the mortal frame into heavenly life. But it is only possible for us to enter into this divine relationship as we die to the earthly, the sensuous and the human. We must receive the cleansing, sanctifying and quickening power of the Holy Spirit.

### A pure church

As we consider this third figure, the purifying work of Christ is especially emphasized. It is only possible to enter into this exalted relationship as we meet Jesus in the heart-searching processes of His grace, remembering that He gave Himself for the church "that he might sanctify and cleanse it with the washing of water by the word." Still, the description of the degree of purity Christ would have His church attain continues: ". . . that he might present it to himself a glorious church, not having spot, or wrinkle, or any such thing; but that it should be holy and without blemish."

How the very soul quivers under the white light of this searching sentence! Not a spot must remain. Our garments may be white and clean except for a single speck, but that is fatal. Shall we bring to Him today the single stains, the flaws in the fabric, the specks on the garment?

There must not be a wrinkle. A wrinkle may be the result not of defilement, but of neglect, carelessness, an imperfect work of advancing age and infirmity. A wrinkle in the linen results from careless ironing. A wrinkle in the countenance comes by feebleness. We must not only be pure, but we must be vigorous. We must be in full spiritual strength. We must have no marks of negligence, but be up to the standard of His holy will.

Still finer is the last phrase, "any such thing." There may be clouds upon the finished surface, dinginess, shades, faint suggestions of a fault or a flaw. His love demands that these must go, and so He touches again, and in His faithfulness works out the inward processes of His inexorable grace. One day, with a pride and joy far greater than our own, He shall present us to Himself, a glorious bride, not having spot or wrinkle, or any such thing, while the wondering universe cries out: "Come and let us see the bride, the Lamb's wife."

It is said that once a young man of noble birth wedded a country girl to whom he had been engaged since childhood. But he forgot that in the interval he had grown beyond her through the influence of higher education and worldwide travel. He never realized until their lives were linked indissolubly together that it was impossible for her to understand him or enter into the higher meaning of his life. He loved her dearly, treated her chivalrously, but pined and died of a broken heart because there never could be companionship.

Beloved, Christ has betrothed you to Him. You are to spend eternity in His palaces and on His throne. You are to be the companion and partner of His mightiest enterprises in the ages to come. Perhaps with Him you are to colonize a constellation of space and govern the boundless universe of God. Do you know that He is educating you now to be a fit companion for such a kingdom? Will you let Him love you all He wants to and fit you for such a destiny as will some day fill you with everlasting wonder and adoration?

# The Logic of Missions

*"The Logic of Missions" (from Missionary Messages) reveals the burning drive in the heart of Simpson that resulted in The Christian and Missionary Alliance. It is one of Simpson's best convention sermons. It stirred his audience then, and now after almost a century, it stirs the modern reader. To this man of God, world evangelization was not a great cause, but a command that no thinking Christian could deny. The self-sacrifice and self-denial of those who carry out the Great Commission is rational. Arguing from the fact of man's lostness and the splendor of God's plan for redemption, Simpson concludes that the church has but one option: an immediate and all-out endeavor to finish the work.*

*How then shall they call on him in whom they have not believed? and how shall they believe in him of whom they have not heard? and how shall they hear without a preacher? And how shall they preach, except they be sent? as it is written, How beautiful are the feet of them that preach the gospel of peace, and bring glad tidings of good things! (Romans 10:14–15).*

P AUL'S CHAIN OF INEXORABLE logic, preserved for us
in Romans 10:14–15, sums up the whole practical
side of missions. It brings home the guilt of the
world's moral, spiritual and eternal ruin to the conscience of every man and woman who is not doing his
or her best to send the gospel of Jesus Christ to all
mankind.

There is no sentiment about this. It is stern, un-
yielding logic, and it brings every one of us, by an
irresistible argument, face to face with the responsibility of the world's ruin or redemption. It tells us that
God has provided a remedy sufficient and completely
fitted for all the wants of our fallen race. He has given
us a salvation that is adequate, adapted and designed
for all the world. He has put the simple conditions of
it within the reach of every person who hears the
gospel. Now, to use an expressive colloquial phrase,
"it is up to you"—and me—whether people shall be
lost or saved. Let us look at this magnificent argument.

Paul always begins with the heart. He starts with a
great burst of love for his lost brethren. "Brethren, my
heart's desire and prayer to God for Israel is, that they
might be saved" (Romans 10:1). This is the motivating
power of missionary work—a heart aflame with love
for people and a longing to lead them to Christ.

**The gospel for the world**

But mere sentiment cannot save a lost world. The
tenderest love and most self-denying sacrifices cannot
lift our lost humanity from the fearful effects of the
Fall. It needs a divine remedy, a gospel of superhuman
power as well as divine compassion.

The Apostle Paul had discovered such a gospel and

had been commissioned to declare to men such a remedy. This remedy and gospel were so incomparably superior to all that the world had found, up to that point in time, that he was enthusiastic in his desire to proclaim it to all men.

He had found a panacea for all human sin and sorrow, and it was so good that he could not bear to have a single human being miss it. He expressed it by one great word which was a favorite of his and which we find again and again in his epistle to the Romans. It is the word "righteousness." Earlier in his letter, in a well-known passage, he put it this way: "But now the righteousness of God without the law is manifested" (Romans 3:21). Later he expressed the idea again: "Christ is the end of the law for righteousness to every one that believeth" (10:4). That fine expression, "righteousness," means rightness. The idea is that God has provided a plan for righting every wrong of humanity.

It was said of the apostles, "These that have turned the world upside down are come hither" (Acts 17:6). There is a story told of an eccentric English evangelist who took that text for one of his open-air sermons in a new place. He began by saying, "First, the world is wrong side up. Second, the world must be turned upside down. Third, we are the men to set it right." In the man's quaint phrases, this is really the purpose of the gospel. It is God's way of making things right.

Things are wrong between the world and God. The world does not know Him. Its citizens do not love Him. They do not trust Him. They cannot stand before Him with acceptance. Their sins have separated them from God, and the guilt of sin is bearing them down to deeper sin and a dark eternal hell. But God has sent Jesus Christ to make this right. He has become a Man and as such represents the fallen human family. As the great representative Man, He has taken upon Himself man's sins, man's obligations, man's wrongs against God. He has met the issue, and He has paid the penalty. He has lived up to the requirements of God's most perfect law and has thus wrought out a righteousness that is perfect and sufficient to cover all the guilt of fallen man and forever to settle the salvation of every sinner who will accept this settlement. This is the gospel of salvation through the blood and righteousness of Jesus Christ. It is the only remedy for a guilty conscience and a sinful heart. It is the power of God unto salvation to everyone that believes, and it was Paul's delight to go to the known world and tell sinful men of the glorious righteousness of God.

But it is more than this. It is also God's provision for taking away the sin of the human heart and giving to weak, fallen man the power to be right toward God and toward all men. The worst thing in our fallen state is not our guilt and our liability to eternal punishment. The worst thing is our helplessness to do right or even want to do right. Men tell us that the heathen will be saved if they will live up to the light they have. We do not stop to question this, for God will surely do right by every righteous man. But the difficulty is that the heathen cannot do right of themselves. We — with the gospel light — cannot do right. Human nature is helpless, and the very essence of the gospel is that it gives the power to choose and do the right. It takes away the love of sin; it makes us love the things that God loves and hate the things He hates. It has power to cleanse, purify and uplift human nature. It is a divine force placed within the human heart, that causes us to walk in His statutes and keep His commandments. This is the very thing we are called to give to a lost world: the righteousness of God. This is the glory of the gospel, and with such a remedy for the dark stains of humanity, what a cruel crime it is to keep it back from our struggling and sinking fellow man.

## All this comes through Christ

This righteousness is not character slowly built up. It is not mere merit painfully attained as the Buddhist tries to attain it. It is a Person, a living, loving, real Man, Christ, our Brother, our Savior, our living Head, who has fashioned it all out for us and who waits to give it to us the moment we accept Him. It is not a struggle to be good in our own strength, but a simple act of confidence in a loving Redeemer who undertakes the whole task for us and gives to us a free gift of righteousness the moment we accept Him.

Christ is the world's answer, the world's remedy, the world's hope, the world's Redeemer. The apostle's one business was to minister Christ to men and women, to tell them of Jesus and bring them into contact with Him who is the desire of the nations and the remedy for all man's wrongs. All this is without the law and by the free grace of God. "Christ is the end of the law for righteousness to every one that believeth" (Romans 10:4).

When we receive Him, we pass from under the condemnation, the claims, the terrors of the law. We do not have to obey a stern commandment as a condition of salvation, but we receive a righteousness, higher than man himself could ever have attained, as the free gift of His grace. His merits become ours, and we stand before God in as good a place as if we had never sinned, in as good a place as if we had done everything that He has done and kept every commandment that He has kept. Not only so, we receive Him into our hearts as a living Presence, an efficient Power, a divine Enabling, and united to Him we can relive the life He lived and be even as He was in this world.

Such a salvation, so complete, so sufficient, so far-reaching, so free, is enough to set on fire the hearts of angels and to make us human beings who have received it burn with desire to pass it on to all the race. What a pity that this lost world should be another hour without it.

This righteousness is accessible and available to all people. It is not far off, but near. It is not hung high in the heavens where sinners must painfully climb the heights of virtue and achievement before they can attain it, but it reaches down to the level of the most lost and helpless of men. Its terms are as simple as language can express or love can provide. It says, "Whosoever shall call on the name of the Lord shall be saved" (Acts 2:21). There is nothing so easy as to call, to utter a cry of need and know that instantly the love and grace of God will respond. It is not restricted to any class or race: "There is no difference . . . for the same Lord over all is rich unto all that call upon him" (Romans 10:12). It is not for moral Jew or cultivated Greek or initiated philosopher, but it is for the common people, the sinful people, the "whosoever will."

He uses a beautiful figure to express its accessibility

*Say not in thine heart, Who shall ascend into heaven?*

*(that is, to bring Christ down from above:) Or, Who shall descend into the deep? (that is, to bring up Christ again from the dead.) But what saith it? The word is nigh thee, even in thy mouth, and in thy heart: that is, the word of faith, which we preach; that if thou shalt confess with thy mouth the Lord Jesus, and shalt believe in thine heart that God hath raised him from the dead, thou shalt be saved (Romans 10:6–9).*

A person does not need to slowly climb to some high experience to be able to know God and become righteous, as the ancient philosophers taught. He does not need to go down to some depth of abasement to make himself worthy of God's mercy. All the efforts which heathenism inflicts upon its votaries as a meritorious cause of salvation are foolish and needless. Just where the repentant sinner is this moment, he can meet Jesus and sing: "This uttermost salvation, / It reaches me."

Even amid all the wreck of humanity, there is still in every human heart some echo of the voice of God, some sense of need, some responsive touch that the gospel awakens, meets and satisfies. There is a description in Exodus of the nearness of God to sinful people. It comes at the close of chapter 20, immediately after the sublime and awful picture of Mt. Sinai and the terrors of the ancient law. Just at the foot of that fiery mount of judgment, God provided the Israelites with an example of His grace, full of the very spirit of the gospel. It was an altar of earth representing the place where sinful men were to meet the God of this fiery law. They could not meet Him on the fearful top of Sinai, for that only spoke of judgment. But this altar of earth represented the cross of Calvary and the plan of salvation through the blood of Jesus Christ. There they were to bring their bleeding sacrifices and find atonement for the sin which the law so fearfully condemned.

The description of the altar is a very poem of grace. First, it was to be built not of stone but of earth, the commonest, least expensive material within the reach of everybody. Second, if it was to be made of stone, it must be of stones as they were found, for God said, "If thou lift up thy tool upon it, thou hast polluted it" (v. 25). No works of man must mingle with the free grace which insists upon saving us alone.

Also, there were to be no steps leading up to the altar. There is not a single step needed to raise the sinner to a level where God can meet him. God meets each one on his own level, stooping to the lowest place where guilty sinners exist, crying, "Ho, every one that thirsteth, come ye to the waters, and he that hath no money; come ye, buy and eat; . . . without money and without price" (Isaiah 55:1).

There is another beautiful picture of the nearness of God's mercy and grace to helpless sinners in Leviticus 14. It is the picture of the poor leper outside the camp, excluded from the fellowship of his brethren by his uncleanness and leprosy. But in infinite tenderness and mercy, God is represented as going out to meet the sinner there: "the priest shall go forth to him out of the camp" (v. 3). God's mercy meets him where he lies in his separation and misery and supplies all that is necessary for his return and his future way.

Perhaps there has never been a finer illustration of the far-reaching mercy and grace of God to sinful men than that spoken by a poor Chinese. When asked why he had given up Confucius and Buddha and accepted Jesus Christ instead, he said: "I was down in a deep pit into which I had fallen in my folly and sin. I was sinking in the mire and vainly calling for aid. Suddenly a shadow fell across the pit. Looking up, I saw Confucius. I implored him to reach out his hand and help me, but he proceeded calmly to instruct me in the principles of right living, and told me that if I had only listened to his teaching I would not have been there. It was vain for me to cry, 'Help me, help me now! Your good advice will be useful after I get out, but it is useless until someone delivers me from this pit of death,' for he was gone, and I knew that Confucius could not save me.

Later, another shadow fell upon the opening, and I looked up to see Buddha. With the frenzy of despair, I cried to him to save me. But Buddha folded his arms and looked serenely down upon me. 'My son,' he said, 'be quiet, be patient, be still. Don't mind your troubles, ignore them; the secret of happiness is to die to self and surroundings, to retire to the inward calm and center of your heart. There you shall find Nirvana, eternal rest, and that is the end of all existence.' As he turned to leave, I cried, 'Father, if you will only get me out of this pit, I can do all you tell me. But how can I be quiet and satisfied sinking in this awful mire?' He benignly waved his hands and said, 'My son be still, be still,' and passed on. And I knew that Buddha would not save me.

"At that point I was ready to give up hope, when a third shadow fell across my vision. I looked up and saw a Man, like myself, with kind and tender countenance. Marks of dried blood were upon his brow. He spoke to me and said, 'My child, I have come to save you. Will you let me?' I cried out in my despair,

'Come, Lord, help me, I perish!' In a moment He had leaped down into the pit and put His arms around me. He lifted me up, placed me on the brink and took from me my torn and spattered garments. He washed me and robed me in new raiment, and then He said, 'I have come to save you from your distress, and now if you will follow Me, I will never leave you. I will be your Guide and Friend all the way and will keep you from ever falling again.' His name was Jesus. Need I say I fell at His feet, saying, 'Lord, I will follow Thee.'

"That," said the man, "is why I became a Christian."

This same Jesus who has brought you and me out of a horrible pit and the miry clay and set our feet upon solid rock and established our goings, is longing to do the same for every lost and helpless child of our fallen race. How sad, how needless, how terrible that we should allow them to perish without ever knowing Him. How can we be so cruel to them and so heartless to Him? By the love that ransomed us, let us go, like Him, "to seek and to save that which was lost." Such is the glorious gospel which God has provided for this lost world.

## Our responsibility for giving the gospel to the world

There are three links in this chain of responsibility.

1. "How shall they call on him in whom they have not believed?" Believing is the responsibility of every sinner. God calls upon every lost man to believe on the Lord Jesus Christ, to call upon Him as Savior and Lord. If people refuse to do this, the responsibility for the loss of their souls is their own. They have had their chance and they have made their choice. God cannot save people without their believing in Him.

In the very nature of things there must be confidence, there must be consent, there must be response of the human will and the human heart to the call of God. Salvation is not a mechanical process, but a voluntary one. Every human effort must cooperate with God. "He that believeth on him is not condemned: but he that believeth not is condemned already, because he hath not believed in the name of the only begotten Son of God" (John 3:18). Men deserve to be lost forever if they refuse to accept the Savior who is offered to them. This is the one deciding question for every human being. No person will perish eternally on account of his sins but only on account of his treatment of Jesus Christ. It is not the sin question but the Son question. Because of that, God wants the message of salvation offered to all mankind. Then the responsibility rests with them. "Go ye into all the world, and preach the gospel to every creature. He that believeth and is baptized shall be saved; but he that believeth not shall be damned" (Mark 16:15–16).

2. The second link of responsibility is the human agency. "How shall they believe in him of whom they have not heard? And how shall they hear without a preacher?" The agency is the messenger. God has ordained the human agency as the conveyor of the gospel to mankind. He might have proclaimed it with trumpet voice, as He doubtless did when He went down into Hades and preached to the spirits in prison. He might have written it in flaring characters upon the sky. He might have sent a thousand angels to declare it among the nations. But He has chosen to give us the privilege and honor of sharing with Him in this glorious work. "Now then we are ambassadors for Christ, as though God did beseech you by us: we

pray you in Christ's stead, be ye reconciled to God" (2 Corinthians 5:20). Therefore, Christ's first word to His disciples is "go." The call of the heavenly voices is, "Whom shall I send, and who will go for us?" (Isaiah 6:8). He is waiting for volunteers, and He will only send volunteers. It is the duty of everyone to go who has not a good reason for staying at home. Have we heard this call? Have we weighed our responsibility? Have we waited for our marching orders? Are we where God wants us in this matter? Young men and women, fathers and mothers, students and earnest people of every name who are standing at the cross-road of life, listen today, while again He calls, "Whom shall I send, and who will go for us?" God grant that many may answer, even today: "Here am I, Lord, send me."

3. The last link brings the responsibility home to every one of us. "How shall they preach except they be sent?" Sending is something that we all can do. Certainly, it is God's business to send a messenger, and the words *apostle* and *missionary* just mean "sent ones." The 12 apostles were 12 missionaries, and every missionary should be sent by the Holy Spirit.

But it is our duty to send them too. We read in Acts that before God began the great work of modern missions, He commanded the church at Antioch to separate its two best leaders and send them forth as foreign missionaries—and it is distinctly added, "So they, being sent forth by the Holy Spirit, departed unto . . . Cyprus" (13:4). Who is to do the sending? First, the church, through its officers and missionary boards is called upon to send. And, the missionary call should always have two sides—the volunteer's side, as he offers his services, and the church's side, as it accepts him and stands with him in joint responsibility for his work and for his support.

But the parent can also send his or her child. What are you doing as parents? How are you shaping the future of your children? Are you saying, as one of our missionaries once reported an American Christian as saying to him, "Yes we believe our children should go as missionaries when God calls them, but we do not agitate the question." Is that loyalty to God? Or are you going further? Are you like the eagle that stole the lamb of sacrifice from the altar and found, when she reached her nest, that she had carried a coal from the fire along with the lamb, which in a moment burned up her nest and her young? Have you found that in robbing God of some precious life, you have wrecked that life and desolated your own home circle?

We can also support, financially, those we send. The question of money is today the deciding factor in connection with any large advance movement in the missionary field. We at home can be missionaries just as truly as our brethren are missionaries on the field. God will count our work a partnership with them, and we shall share alike in the recompense when the great harvest shall be gathered.

Are we doing our part? Shall we do it again today to send the missionaries who bring the missing link, the touch of a human hand, the sound of a human voice, the Word of God and the voice of love to wake up the faith of the world's lost children?

A man once called on a Christian businessman, and finding him intensely busy, asked how many hours he worked daily. "Oh," said the man, "24." "How is that possible?" asked his friend. "Why, you see it is this way," he replied. "When I was a young man, I gave my life to God for the foreign mission field. Soon after this, my father died, and it became necessary for me to remain at home and carry on the business for the support of my mother and sister. I have found another way, though, of carrying out my missionary consecration. We have branches of our business in various parts of this country, and this gave me the idea of having a missionary department and branches in various parts of the world. Here, for example, is a map of China, and at that little town in South China is one of our missionary branches. Out in India there is another and another in Africa. So while I am working 12 hours here, my representatives in the missionary branches are sleeping. When I retire at night they begin work on the other side of the world. So you see, our business stays open 24 hours a day. I find that these missionary branches not only give a broader scope to our business but a delightful interest. The very best of all our returns come from them."

That is missionary consecration put into practice. That is the meaning of a missionary pledge. We do not give on the impulse of the moment, then forget about it for 12 months. No, we must enter into a contract that runs the entire year. We carry on our business and perform our daily tasks in partnership with the Lord Jesus Christ, gaining, saving and sacrificing the fruits of our toil for the spread of the gospel and the building up of His glorious kingdom.

CHAPTER

## 10

# The Pattern Prayer

*"The Pattern Prayer" (from* The Life of Prayer*) is replete with practical thoughts from Jesus' model prayer. Simpson believed that the Lord's Prayer was a prayer designed to teach his followers how to pray. "The Pattern Prayer" is a good example of Simpson's style of exposition. While giving careful attention to every detail of the biblical text, he skillfully dresses the homelitical mechanics with a practical and easily understood lesson on prayer. One senses that the author was personally acquainted with the life of prayer.*

*And he said unto them, When ye pray, say, Our Father which art in heaven, Hallowed be thy name. Thy kingdom come. Thy will be done, as in heaven, so in earth. Give us day by day our daily bread. And forgive us our sins; for we also forgive every one that is indebted to us. And lead us not into temptation; but deliver us from evil (Luke 11:2–4).*

THE MODEL PRAYER Jesus taught His disciples was dictated by our Lord in reply to a request from them, "Lord, teach us to pray." His answer was to bid them pray. This is the only way we shall ever learn to pray—by just beginning to do it. As the babbling child learns the art of speech by speaking, and as the lark mounts up to the heights of the sky by beating its

*123*

wings again and again upon the air, so prayer teaches us how to pray. The more we pray, the more we shall learn the mysteries and heights and depths of prayer. And the more we pray, the more we shall realize the incomparable completeness of this that we call the Lord's Prayer. It is the prayer of universal Christendom, the common liturgy of the church of God. It is the earliest and holiest recollection of every Christian child and often the last utterance of the departing saint. We who have used it most have come to feel that there is no want which it does not interpret and no holy aspiration which it may not express. There is nothing else in the Scriptures which more fully evolves the great principles that underlie the divine philosophy of prayer.

## Prayer to the Father

The Lord's Prayer teaches us that all true prayer begins in the recognition of the Father. It is not the cry of nature to an unknown God, but the intelligent converse of a child with his heavenly Father. It presupposes that the suppliant has become a child, and it assumes that the mediation of the Son has preceded the revelation of the Father. No one, therefore, can truly pray this prayer until he or she has accepted the Lord Jesus Christ as Savior, received through Him the child-heart in regeneration and been led into the realization of relationship in the family of God.

The Person to whom prayer is directly addressed is the Father, not the Son or the Holy Spirit. The great purpose of Christ's mediation is to bring us to God and reveal Him to us as our Father in reconciliation and fellowship. The name suggests the spirit of confidence, and this is essential to prayer.

The first attribute of God seen in the Lord's Prayer is not His majesty but His paternal love. To the listening disciples, this must have been a strange concept. They had never heard God so named, at least in His relation to the individual. The Father of the Nation, he was sometimes called, but no Jew had ever dared to call God Father. The disciples had no doubt heard their Master speak of God as His Father, but that they should call Jehovah by such a name was beyond their thinking. But that is what it really means: we may and should recognize that God is our Father in the very sense in which He is Jesus' Father. We have partaken of Jesus' Sonship and His Name; therefore, God becomes our Father. The Name expresses personal and tender love, protection, care and intimacy. It gives to prayer, at the very outset, the beautiful atmosphere of the home circle and the affectionate and intimate fellowship therein.

Have we thus learned to pray? Do wondering angels look down upon our closet every day to see humble and sinful creatures of the dust talking to the majestic Sovereign of the skies? Can it be said to us, "I write unto you, little children, because ye have known the Father?" (1 John 2:13).

## Prayer recognizes the power of God

The model prayer teaches us that prayer should recognize the majesty and almightiness of God. The words, "who art in heaven," or, rather, "who art in the heavens," are intended to convey for the Divine Being a very definite and local personality. God is not a vague influence or pantheistic presence, but a distinct Person, exalted above matter and nature. He has a specific habitation, to which the mind is directed and where He occupies the throne of actual sovereignty over all the universe. He is also recognized as above our level. He is in the heavens, higher than our little world and exalted above all other elements and forces that need His controlling power. It enthrones Him in the place of highest power, authority and glory.

True prayer must ever recognize at once the nearness and greatness of God. The Old Testament is full of the sublimest representation of the majesty of God, and the more fully we realize His greatness, the more boldly will we dare to seek and claim through prayer His intervention in all our trials and emergencies.

As we bow our knees in prayer, we are talking with Him Who still says as He said to Abraham, "I am El Shaddai, the Almighty God"; He says in the words he spoke to Jeremiah, "I am the Lord, the God of all flesh: is there any thing too hard for me?" (Jeremiah 32:27). He declares, as He declared to Isaiah, "Hast thou not known? hast thou not heard, that the everlasting God, the Lord, the Creator of the ends of the earth, fainteth not, neither is weary? there is no searching of his understanding" (Isaiah 40:28).

### Prayer is fellowship with God

The pattern prayer teaches us that prayer is not only a fellowship with God but a fellowship of human hearts. "Our Father" lifts each of us at once out of ourselves and makes us members one of another. Of course, the first link in the fellowship is Christ, our Elder Brother. There is no person, however isolated, but who may come with this prayer in perfect truthfulness and, hand in hand with Christ, say, "Christ's and mine." But it chiefly refers to the fellowship of human hearts. The highest promises are made to those who agree — "symphonize," the Greek says — on earth. There is no place where we can love our friends so beautifully or so purely as at the throne of grace. There is no exercise in which the differences of Christians melt away so completely as when their hearts meet together in the unity of prayer. There is no remedy for the divisions of Christianity but to come closer to the Father. Then, of necessity, we shall be in touch with each other.

## Prayer is worship

This pattern prayer teaches us that worship is the highest element in prayer. "Hallowed be thy name" is more important than any petition in the Lord's Prayer. It brings us directly to God Himself and makes His glory supreme, above all our thoughts and all our wants. It reminds us that the first purpose of our prayers should ever be, not the supply of our personal needs, but the worship and adoration of our God. In the ancient feasts, everything was first brought to God, and then it was given to the worshiper, in several cases, for his use. Its use was hallowed by the fact that it had already been laid at Jehovah's feet. The person who can truly utter this prayer and fully enter into its meaning can also receive all the other petitions of it with double blessing. Not until we have first become satisfied with God Himself and have realized that His glory is above all our desires and interests are we prepared to receive any other blessing. When we can truly say, "Hallowed be thy name whatever comes to me," we will have the substance of all blessing in our heart.

We cannot enter this Holy of Holies without becoming conscious of the hallowing blessing that falls upon and fills us with the glory that we have ascribed to him. The sacred sense of God's overshadowing, the deep and penetrating solemnity and the heavenly calm that fills the person who can truly utter these sacred words, constitute a blessing above all other blessings that even this prayer can ask.

Have we learned to begin our prayer in this holy place, on this heavenly plane? If so, we have learned to pray.

## Prayer and the kingdom

Christ's prayer teaches us that true prayer recognizes the establishment of the kingdom of God as the chief purpose of the divine will and the supreme desire of every true Christian. More than for our own temporal or even spiritual needs, we are to pray for the establishment of that kingdom. This implies that the real remedy for all that needs prayer is the restoration of the kingdom of God. The true cause of all human trouble is that mankind is out of the divine order. The world is in rebellion against its rightful Sovereign. Not until that kingdom is reestablished in every heart and in all the world, can the blessings which prayer desires be realized. Of course, it includes in a primary sense the establishment of the kingdom of God in the individual heart, but much more in the world at large, in fulfillment of God's great purpose of redemption. It is, in short, the prayer for the accomplishment of redemption and its glorious consummation in the coming of our Lord and the setting up of His millennial kingdom. What an exalted view this gives of prayer! How it raises us above our petty selfish cares and cries!

A story is told of a devoted minister who, when

told he was dying and had only half an hour to live, asked his attendants to raise him from his bed and place him on his knees. He then spent the last half-hour of his life in one ceaseless prayer for the evangelization of the world. Truly that was a glorious place to end a life of prayer!

Must it not be true that the failure of many of our prayers can be traced to their selfishness? Is not most of our prayer time spent upon our own interests? What have we ever asked for the kingdom of our Lord? There is no blessing so great as that which comes when our hearts are lifted out of ourselves and become one with Christ in intercession for others and for His cause. There is no joy so pure as that of taking the burden of our Master's cause on our hearts. We should bear it with Him every day in ceaseless prayer, as though its interests wholly depended upon the uplifting of our hands and the remembrance of our faith.

Have we prayed for Jesus' petition as much as we have for our own? There is no ministry which will bring more blessing upon the world and from which we ourselves will reap a larger harvest of eternal fruit than the habit of praying for the progress of Christ's kingdom. We should pray for the needs of His church and work, for His ministers and servants and especially for the evangelization of the neglected peoples who know not how to pray for themselves. Let us awaken from our spiritual selfishness and learn the meaning of the petition, "Thy kingdom come!"

## Prayer: the will of God

Our Lord's prayer teaches us that true prayer is founded upon the will of God as its limitation and encouragement. It is not asking for things because we want them. The primary condition of all true prayer is the renunciation of our own wills so that we may desire and receive God's will instead. Having made the will of our Father the standard of our desires and petitions, we are to claim these petitions with a force and tenacity as great as the will of God itself. This petition, then, instead of being a limitation of prayer, is really a confirmation of our faith, and it gives us the right to claim that the petition thus conformed to His will shall be imperatively fulfilled.

There is no prayer so mighty, so sure, so full of blessing, as this little sentence at which so many of us have often trembled, "Thy will be done." It is not the death-knell of all our happiness, but the pledge of all possible blessing. If it is the will of God to bless us, we shall be blessed. Happy are they who suspend their desires until they know their Father's will, and then ask according to His will. They can rise to the height of His own mighty promise, "If ye abide in me, and my words abide in you, ye shall ask what ye will, and it shall be done unto you" (John 15:7). "Thus saith the Lord, . . . Ask me of things to come concerning my sons, and concerning the work of my hands command ye me" (Isaiah 45:11). What more can we ask of ourselves and others than that God's highest will shall be fulfilled?

How shall we know that will? At the very least, we may always know it by His Word and promise. We may be very sure we are not transcending its infinite bounds if we ask anything that is covered by a promise of His Holy Word. We may immediately turn that promise into an order on the very Bank of Heaven and claim its fulfillment by all the power of His omnipotence and the sanctions of His faithfulness. The added clause itself, "as it is in heaven," implies that the fulfillment of this petition would change earth into a heaven and bring heaven into every one of our lives. This petition, while it implies a spirit of absolute submission, rises to the heights of illimitable faith.

Have we then understood it and learned thus to pray, "Thy will be done in earth, as it is in heaven"?

## Prayer is trusting for every need

The pattern prayer teaches us that prayer may include all our natural and temporal wants and should be accompanied by the spirit of trustful dependence upon our Father's care for the supply of all our earthly needs. "Give us this day our daily bread," gives to every child of God the right to claim a Father's supporting and providing love. It is wonderful to see how much spiritual blessing we may receive by praying and trusting for our temporal needs. They who try, through second causes or through ample human provision, to be independent of God's direct interposition and care, greatly curtail the fullness of their spiritual life. And they also separate God's personal providence from the most simple and minute of life's secular interests. We are to recognize every means of support and temporal link of blessing as directly from His hand. We are to commit every interest of business and life to His direction and blessing.

At the same time, it is implied that there must be in this a spirit of simplicity and daily trust. It is not the bread of future days we ask, but the bread of today. Nor is it always luxurious bread, the bread of affluence—the banquet, the feast. It is daily bread, or rather, as the best authorities translate it, "sufficient bread"—bread such as He sees to be really best for us.

It may not be always bread and butter; it may be homely bread, and it may be sometimes scant bread, but He can make even that sufficient. He can add such a blessing with it and such an impartation of His life and strength as will make us know, like our Master in the wilderness, that "man shall not live by bread alone, but by every word that proceedeth out of the mouth of God" (Matthew 4:4). It implies, in short, a spirit of contentment and satisfaction with our daily lot and a trust that leaves tomorrow's needs in His wise and faithful hand. Our Father will care for us day by day as each new morrow comes.

Have we thus learned to pray for temporal things, bringing all our life to God? Have we learned to come in the spirit of daily trust and thankful contentment with our simple lot and our Father's wisdom and faithfulness?

## Prayer and divine mercy

The Lord's Prayer teaches us that true prayer must always recognize the need for the mercy of God. There are two versions of this petition, "Forgive us our trespasses," and "Forgive us our debts." This is not accidental. We may honestly be conscious of no willful or known disobedience or sin. And yet there may be infinite debt, omission and shortcoming as compared with the high standard of God's holiness and even our own ideal. If we are sensitive and thoroughly quickened in spirit, we will never reach a place where we are not aware of so much more to which we are reaching out and to which God is pressing us forward. We will need to say, "Forgive us our debts," even when perhaps we cannot conscientiously say, "Forgive us our transgressions."

This sense of demerit on our part throws us constantly upon the merits and righteousness of our great High Priest. It makes our prayers forever dependent on His intercession and offered in His name. Jesus enables the most unworthy of us to "come boldly unto the throne of grace [to] obtain mercy, and find grace to help in time of need" (Hebrews 4:16). We do not mean that the Lord expects us to be constantly sinning and repenting, for the final petition of this prayer is for complete deliverance from all evil. But He graciously grades the prayer to cover every experience from that of the most sanctified to the humble but guilty penitent.

This petition presupposes a solemn spirit of forgiveness in the heart of the suppliant. Such is indispensable if the suppliant is to receive forgiveness. The Greek construction and the use of the aorist tense express a very practical shade of meaning, namely that the forgiveness of the injury that has been done to us has preceded our prayer for divine forgiveness. Freely translated, it should read, "Forgive us our trespasses as we have already forgiven them that trespassed against us."

There are certain spiritual requisites that are indispensable to acceptable prayer, even for the simplest mercies. Without them we cannot pray. The person who is filled with bitterness cannot approach God in communion. Inferentially, the person who is cherishing any other sin is likewise hindered from access to the throne of grace. This is an Old Testament truth that all the abundant grace of the New Testament has neither revoked nor weakened. "If I regard iniquity in my heart, the Lord will not hear me" (Psalm 66:18), was a lesson which even David learned from sad and

solemn experience. "I will wash mine hands in inno-
cency: so will I compass thine altar" (Psalm 26:6) is
the eternal condition of acceptable communion with
the Holy One. The most sinful may come for mercy,
but they must put away their sin and freely forgive the
trespasses of others. There seem to be two unpardon-
able sins. One is the sin which willfully rejects the
Holy Spirit and the Savior presented by Him—the sin
of willful unbelief. The other is the sin of unforgiv-
ingness.

## The protection of prayer

The model prayer teaches us that prayer is our true
weapon and safeguard in the temptations of life, and
that we may rightly claim the divine protection from
our spiritual adversaries. This petition, "Lead us not
into temptation," undoubtedly covers the whole field
of our spiritual conflicts. It may be interpreted, in the
largest sense, as all we need to arm us against our
spiritual enemies. It cannot strictly mean that we pray
to be kept from all temptation, for God Himself has
said, "Blessed is the man that endureth temptation"
(James 1:12), "Count it all joy when ye fall into divers
temptations" (v. 2) and "Let patience have her perfect
work" (v. 4).

It rather means, "Lead us not into a *crisis* of temptation" or "Lead us so that we shall not *fall* under temptation or be tried above what we are able to bear."
There are spiritual trials and crises which come to
people that are too hard for them to bear—snares into
which many of them fall. This is the particular promise which this prayer claims. They shall not come into
any such crisis; they shall be kept out of situations
which would be overwhelming. It is a promise that

will carry them through the places which would be too dangerous and keep them safe from peril.

This is what is meant by the verse "The Lord knoweth how to deliver the godly out of temptations" (2 Peter 2:9a). Another even more gracious promise is found in First Corinthians 10:13: "There hath no temptation taken you but such as is common to man: but God is faithful, who will not suffer you to be tempted above that ye are able; but will with the temptation also make a way to escape, that ye may be able to bear it." When we think how many there are who perish through yielding to temptation, and how narrow the path often is, what comfort it should give us to know that our Lord has authorized us to claim His divine protection. In these awful perils, He enables us to meet the wiles of the devil and insidious foes against whom all our own skill would be unavailing!

This was the master's own solemn admonition to His disciples in the garden during the struggle with the powers of darkness: "Watch and pray, that ye enter not into temptation" (Matthew 26:41). And this was His own safeguard in that hour. The apostle has given it to us as the unceasing prescription of wisdom and safety in connection with our spiritual conflict: "Praying always with all prayer and supplication in the Spirit, and watching thereunto with all perseverance and supplication for all saints" (Ephesians 6:18). "Continue in prayer, and watch in the same with thanksgiving" (Colossians 4:2).

### Prayer and sanctification

The crowning petition of the Lord's Prayer is a request for entire sanctification, including deliverance from every other form of evil. "Deliver us from evil." This has frequently been translated "from the evil one," but the neuter gender contradicts this and renders it most natural to translate it, as the old version does, from evil in all forms rather than from the author of evil. This is more satisfying to Christian experience. There are many forms of evil which do not come from the evil one. We have as much cause to pray against ourselves as against the devil. And there are physical evils covered by this petition as well as spiritual temptations. It is a petition, therefore, against sin, sickness and sorrow in every form in which they could be evils.

It is a prayer for our complete deliverance from all the effects of the Fall, in spirit, soul and body. It is a prayer which echoes the fourfold gospel and the fullness of Jesus in the highest and widest measure. It teaches us that we may expect victory over the power of sin, support against the attacks of sickness, triumph over all sorrow and a life in which all things shall be only good and work together for good according to God's high purpose. Surely the prayer of the Holy Spirit for such a blessing is the best pledge of the answer! Let us not be afraid to claim it in all its fullness.

**Prayer and praise**

All prayer should end with praise and believing confidence. The Lord's Prayer, according to the best manuscripts, really ends with "Deliver us from evil," but later copies contain the closing clause, "For thine is the kingdom, and the power, and the glory for ever. Amen." While it is extremely doubtful that our Lord uttered these words as the conclusion of His model prayer, yet they have so grown into the phraseology of Christendom that we may, without danger, draw from them our closing lessons.

The doxology expresses the spirit of praise and consecration. We ascribe to God the authority and power to do what we have asked. We give glory to His name. Then, in token of our confidence that He will do so, we add the Amen, which simply means, "So let it be done." In fact, it is faith ascending to the throne. It is faith humbly claiming and commanding, in the name of Jesus, that for which humility has petitioned. Our Lord requires this element of faith and this acknowledgment and attestation of His faithfulness as a condition of answered prayer. No prayer is complete therefore until faith has added its "Amen."

Such, then, are come of the principal teachings of this universal prayer. How often our lips have uttered it! Let it search our hearts. Let it show us the imperfection, the selfishness, the smallness, the unbelief of what we call prayer. Let us henceforth repeat its pregnant words with deeper thoughtfulness. Let us weigh them with more solemn realization than ever before. May they come to be to us what they indeed are, the summary of all prayer, the expression of all possible need and blessing, the language of a worship like that of the holy ranks who continually surround the throne above. Then indeed shall His kingdom come and His will be done on earth as it is in heaven.

Beautiful and blessed prayer! How it recalls the most sacred associations of life! How it follows the prodigal even in his deepest downfall and his latest moments! How it expands with the deepening spiritual life of the saint! How it wafts the latest aspirations and adorations of the departing Christian to the throne to which he is ready to wing his way! Let it be more dear to us henceforth, more real. Let it be deeper, wider and higher as it teaches us to pray, as it wings our petition to the throne of grace.

And if perchance you are one who has uttered the Lord's Prayer without the right to say "Our Father," may you this very moment stop and think, with tears, of the lips that once taught you its tender accents years ago. Kneel down at the feet of your mother's God, your father's God, your sister's God. If you are willing to say, "Forgive us our trespasses as we forgive those that trespass against us," you may dare to add, linked in everlasting hope with those that first voiced those words to you, "Our Father, which art in heaven."

On a lonely bed in a southern hospital, an old Civil War veteran lay dying. A Christian friend called on him and tried to speak to him about Christ, but the old man repelled him with infidel scorn. After several attempts, the Christian finally just knelt down by the bed and tenderly repeated the Lord's Prayer, slowly and solemnly. When he arose to leave, the infidel's eyes were wet with tears. He tried to brush them away and conceal his feelings, but at last he broke down. "My mother taught me that prayer more than 50 years ago," he said, "and it quite broke me up to hear it again." The Christian left, not wishing to hinder the voice of God. The next time he called, the patient was not there. Sending for the nurse, he asked about the man.

"He died a couple of nights ago," the nurse said. "But just before the end, I heard him repeating the words, 'Our Father who is in heaven.' Then he seemed to add in a husky voice, 'Mother, I am coming! He is *my* Father, too.'"

Dear friend, let this old prayer become to you a holy bond with all that is dearest on earth and a stepping-stone to the very gates of heaven!

# The Discipline of Faith

*In "The Discipline of Faith" (from In the School of Faith), a master teacher and preacher talks about what pleases God. During the fall of 1889 Simpson began preaching a series of messages based on the Old Testament patriarchs. Those sermons were first published under the title "Seven Stars in the Firmament." Jacob is the subject of the chapter called "The Discipline of Faith." Reviewing Jacob's life story, Simpson shows how this master of self-effort became a man of dependent faith. The chastening of God was Jacob's teacher, and his experiences illustrate basic biblical principles for those who seek to live by faith.*

IN SOME WAYS the most illustrious of all the patriarchs—the one who, humanly speaking, gave his name for all time to Israel—was the least noble, the least attractive. Jacob was, in fact, the meanest and most selfish patriarch of all. Twelve hundred years later, the prophet Isaiah speaks of him as the "worm Jacob." The figure well expresses Jacob's insinuating and undermining nature. And yet, out of this wretched material, God made His own great prince to show to poor sinners what grace can do with a person if he or she will but receive its discipline. Let us look at the five chapters of Jacob's history.

## Jacob's choice

Jacob chose the birthright and the blessing which it involved. He set his heart upon the covenant blessing of his race. He was selfish and grasping. He resorted to intrigue to accomplish his purpose. But the one thing which eternally distinguishes Jacob from the earthborn and earthly minded Esau was this: He appreciated and claimed, with every fiber of his being, the great, all-embracing prize of God's covenant promise. In spite of all Jacob's defects, God saw his preference for spiritual things. Jacob thus represents the first germ of the spiritual nature in any soul, the determination of the will, the direction of the heart, the singleness of purpose, the value a man or a woman places on eternal things.

Esau was superficial, transient, earthly minded, hedonistic. His highest good was the present gratification; his horizon stretched only to the setting sun. His deepest desire, his highest aspirations were the instincts, passions, wants of his physical nature. He was impulsively generous, frank and affectionate; but it was an animal instinct. He was the fleshly man. "Behold, I am at the point to die: and what profit shall this birthright do to me?" (Genesis 25:32). That was the very time when faith would have looked out on the eternal profit or claimed that, with such a promise, he should not die till the birthright covenant was fulfilled.

Jacob saw "the land that is very far off," and sprang

to meet it. He sold all that he had for the pearl of great price. He grasped with both hands the priceless blessing his fond mother had often told him of, but whose full significance he might yet only dimly comprehend. But this he knew, that it was linked with all the promises of God and all the hopes of his race.

And God loved him for this choice. The birthright blessing was the mightiest thing in Jacob's life. The mightiest thing in any person's life is a will that sees the heavenly prize and gets its hands upon it to let go no more. Jacob wanted the blessing at any cost. It was this same mighty will which afterward at Peniel held fast to the angel and cried: "I will not let thee go, except thou bless me" (Genesis 32:26).

To choose God, His promise, His inheritance, His blessing and to let heaven and earth pass away before we relinquish the claim is the very essence of faith. It was of this that Jesus said to Martha, "Mary hath chosen that good part, which shall not be taken away from her" (Luke 10:42). It was of this He said to the Syrophonecian woman: "O woman, great is thy faith: be it unto thee even as thou wilt" (Matthew 15:28).

Jacob's faith was not complete. Had it been he would not have begun to work out so cunningly his chosen destiny, but would have trusted God to do what He had promised before his birth. All this he had to slowly and painfully learn. He had to be saved from his scheming, supplanting and restless spirit. But Jacob had the germ, a single aim, a fixed will and a perfect heart toward the covenant blessing, and God could well afford to hew and polish and cut away the rest.

As for Esau, there was nothing to prune and purify. The roots of his nature were all in the world. He had nothing in common with the heart of God. Perhaps he was handsome. Certainly he was generous and largehearted. So is many a dumb creature that knows not God. A noble dog, a generous horse, a fond mother bird are attractive too, but they are only animated clay. For men and women to lift their eyes and hearts no higher is to be lost forever. The world is full of Esaus, fine fellows in their way, but "whose end is destruction, whose God is their belly, . . . who mind earthly things" (Philippians 3:19).

## Jacob's first revelation

Jacob had chosen God, through his mother's teachings, no doubt, and through the simple letter of the Word. But he had not yet seen God for himself. The Most High had not yet spoken to him. He was much like the person who has given himself to Christ on simple faith and choice, but has not yet received any deep experimental sense of eternal things. But the time for this finally came and, as often happens, it came in a dark and trying hour.

Separated for the first time from his home and his mother's tender love, through the consequences of her artifice and his own, Jacob laid his head on a stony pillow (which might well represent the feelings of his heart) and went to sleep. In his dreams, the Lord met him in His first revelation of covenant grace. He dreamed that a ladder appeared on the ground with its top reaching to heaven. It was the fitting figure of his own high purpose. He, too, had set his ladder no lower than the skies, and God met him at the top as the God of Abraham and Isaac. He gave him in covenant the promises he had claimed, pledging to him His constant presence until all His promised will would be finished. "I am with thee, and will keep thee in all places whither thou goest, . . . for I will not leave thee, until I have done that which I have spoken to thee of " (Genesis 28:15).

Jacob awoke with a solemn sense of God's immediate presence, and while his words expressed the deepest reverence and the same inflexible purpose, yet there was all the distance and the dread of the yet unsanctified heart. "How dreadful is this place!" (v. 17) is the language of the soul that does not yet know its sonship. But he was a true servant and knew that his choice was sealed, that the God of Abraham was his Lord, that the covenant blessing had become his own and that the angels of God's providence henceforth encompassed his path.

For us the vision means more than Jacob saw. That ladder is the revelation of Jesus Christ as the heavenly way. Through Him God becomes our covenant Father and all heaven's blessings are made our inheritance. Has our faith claimed the glorious revelation? Have our feet begun to climb the blessed ascent?

### Jacob's consecration at Peniel

More than 20 years passed by, and Jacob had grown little, if any, in his spiritual life. He was just like us all, content in the low plane of spiritual life with which we began. He allowed idolatry to be retained by his wives. He continued to plot and scheme to outwit even the crafty Laban. He accumulated a fortune in herds and flocks. Perhaps his heart had begun to rest in the prosperity of his outward estate.

But God let new troubles gather around him, and, as he returned once more to his old Canaan home, the most terrible peril of his life confronted him. Esau with an armed band was coming to meet him. All the treasured bitterness of a quarter of a century seemed waiting for the opportunity of terrible vengeance. It was the crisis of his life, and all his scheming and shrewdness were insufficient to meet it. Still he did all that tact can do. He sent on a costly present to Esau. He separated his little band in the safest way he could contrive. Then, with a desolate sense of his utter helplessness, he fell at the feet of God.

Again Jacob saw the midnight of life and again the dawn of a brighter morning. The hour of despair became the hour of self-renunciation and divine victory. Alone with God at Jabbok's ford, he wrestled in all the strength of his despair. And when his strength was gone and he sank under the withering touch of the angel's hand, he found the secret of power. He exchanged his strength for God's omnipotence. It was not that the mighty wrestlings of his prayer were wrong—all things are born in the throes of travail—but it was that he should learn that Another than he was wrestling too. "There wrestled a man with him" (Genesis 32:24). And when he yielded himself up to that Presence in the submission of perfect trust, then came the fullness of God's working and God's victorious love. We too must learn that the secret of our deepest desires after God is His own overruling grace. The spring of our mightiest doing and praying must be His doing and praying in us. We need to say with Paul: "I also labour, striving according to his working, which worketh in me mightily" (Colossians 1:29). Jacob rose from that hour a new man: "Thy name shall be called no more Jacob, but Israel: for as a prince hast thou power with God . . . and hast prevailed" (Genesis 32:28).

Not a word was said about Esau or the trouble that had so concerned Jacob before. God did not mention it, and Jacob had lost all thought of it in another Presence. When he had God Himself, he had all things. When we come to the heart of things in God, all our cares and questions flee. God Himself is the answer to them all.

Perhaps the trouble was the occasion that brought us to God. Perhaps we came thinking of little else and with very little thought of Him. But we went away lost in a Presence that bore us and our burden, too. It is well to bring our difficulties, even our very least ones, to Him. An aching finger is as good an occasion to know God as the vastest issue of life. But it is the Blesser and not the blessing, it is the Lord and not the deliverance, that is the real benediction. How often has some commonplace thing become a link to bind us forever to His very throne, forming a chain of communication for infinite blessings. As a little bit of common glass is sufficient to reflect the full glory of the sun, so the smallest trifle has often had room in it for a whole heaven of God's love and help to come to us.

The trouble with Esau had vanished. The brothers met the next day with embraces of affection from spirits that God had touched while Jacob prayed. Could we have seen behind the curtains that night, we would have beheld a sleepless man in his Idumean tent, tossing on his bed as he thought of childhood's memories and fights with bloody purpose of revenge. We might have said it was the impulse of a generous nature that made him spring to his feet and resolve that bygones should be bygones. No! No! It was God. It was prayer and it was the law of faith that binds all hearts to the touch of His hand and the hands that touch His throne.

But this was the least part of it by far. Esau came and went. But Jacob's life moved on, still on that higher plane which began that night. Henceforth He was God's Israel, fit to become the head of the chosen tribes.

How different God was to him after that. God was not at the distant top of the ladder, but near at hand. He had Jacob in His very embrace. He encompassed all of Jacob's future life with His presence and blessing.

Have you come to Peniel? Have you been left alone with Him who encompasses your path and your lying down? Have you received the touch that withers your thigh, that slays your natural strength and confidence, that sends you forth a weak and halting person clothed with no power but God's? Have you seen God face to face? Has He brought the throne of His presence into your heart?

## The discipline of trial

We never know the full meaning of trial until we fully know the Lord. Jacob's severest trials came after his Peniel consecration. Jacob received his blessing. God then took him into the crucible of suffering.

First was the dishonor of his daughter Dinah and the subsequent murder of the Schechemites by his willful sons. This would involve him in future strife with the inhabitants of the land. The whole incident was not so much a trial as it was a punishment for his unjustifiable lingering on forbidden ground. God had sent him back to Canaan, and he had no business tarrying. We cannot remain upon the borders of an evil world without real peril to ourselves and our children.

Immediately after this, God commanded: "Arise, go up to Bethel, and dwell there: and make there an altar unto God" (Genesis 35:1). The house of God and the very gate of heaven was henceforth to be his dwelling place. And so, renewing his consecration and separating himself and his household from every doubtful thing, he went back to the scene of his early blessing. At once, he reared an altar to God.

It was well he did not wait, because great and bitter trials soon began which needed the refuge and support of the divine presence. His beloved Rachel was torn from his side in the pangs of Benjamin's birth. Then Reuben committed an unnatural crime, dishonoring his father's name. And then came the saddest, longest, darkest, strangest trial of all—the loss of Joseph, Rachel's firstborn son. For possibly a quarter of a century, that trial dragged on. Not one ray of light fell on the blackness of Jacob's desolation. After that came the years of famine and the need to buy grain in Egypt. Then came the last drop in Jacob's overflowing cup of trials—the demand that his son Benjamin appear before Egypt's prime minister. It was too much for Jacob to bear. He cried out in agony: "Joseph is not, and Simeon is not, and ye will take Benjamin away: all these things are against me" (Genesis 42:36). But, Jacob could not escape even that bitter drop. All he counted precious on earth he had to put into God's hands. And so he waited for the outcome.

It was enough. The cup was empty at last. And it was filled with a joy so strangely sweet that even Jacob's faith was scarcely able to believe it. To think

that God could have for him, after those years of
bitterness, so great a joy! Not only was Benjamin safe,
but Joseph was alive! Jacob needed the sight of
Joseph's wagons to be convinced that it was true. "It is
enough;" he cried, "Joseph my son is yet alive" (Genesis 45:28). God can be trusted.

> It may be that the future
>     Will be less bitter than you think;
> Or if Marah must be Marah,
>     He will stand beside the brink,
> But it may be He is keeping
>     For the coming of your feet,
> Some gift of such rare blessedness,
>     Some joy so strangely sweet
> That your lips can scarcely utter
>     The thanks you cannot speak.

## The triumph of faith

For Jacob, all the intended evil was overruled by
God's omnipotent wisdom. Out of the darkest of trials, Jacob saw blessing and honor come to his
son Joseph, joy to his own heart, needed instruction
to his wayward sons and food for a world facing famine. Instead of complaining, "All these things are
against me," Jacob could say as he placed his hands on
the heads of Joseph's two sons, "The Angel which
redeemed me from all evil, bless the lads" (Genesis
48:16).

Jacob himself had learned to be still at last. The
eager, active spirit had quieted. With a sense of all it
meant, he could say in his deathbed benediction: "I
have waited for thy salvation, O Lord" (Genesis
49:18). He had learned to wait. His restless heart

was quieted at last. The worm Jacob was perfected through sufferings and able to ascend from the chrysalis of clay to the immortality of glory.

Out of filthy rags, human skill can create exquisite sheets of high-quality paper. These are used for prints of famous paintings, for letters of affection, for Bible texts of comfort and inspiration. So out of the soiled and wrecked remnants of human worthlessness, God is making the tablets on which He loves to write His character, His thoughts and His own glorious image. Jacob glorified God's exceeding and marvelous grace. May we trust Him, too. Then, as Paul puts it in Ephesians 2:9, ". . . in the ages to come he might shew the exceeding riches of his grace in his kindness toward us through Christ Jesus."

# The Righteousness of God

*In "The Righteousness of God" (from* Christ in the Bible — Romans)*, Simpson declares that all is in Christ, who is made unto us righteousness. Simpson's masterful devotional commentary on the book of Romans, like so many other of his works, was compiled from a series of sermons. That accounts for its popular style. Though rich with abundant illustration and real-life application, it does not fail to set forth in precise language the great doctrines of biblical salvation. "The Righteousness of God" lays out the foundations for the whole superstructure of New Testament teaching.*

*But now the righteousness of God without the law is manifested, being witnessed by the law and the prophets; Even the righteousness of God which is by faith of Jesus Christ unto all and upon all them that believe: for there is no difference. For all have sinned, and come short of the glory of God; Being justified freely by his grace through the redemption that is in Christ Jesus. Whom God hath set forth to be a propitiation through faith in his blood, to declare his righteousness for the remission of sins that are past, through the forbearance of*

*God; To declare, I say, at this time his righteousness: that he might be just, and the justifier of him which believeth in Jesus (Romans 3:21–26).*

THERE IS SUCH A THING in human courts as condemning a man to save him. A wise lawyer, when he perceives that his client cannot prove his innocence, will advise him to "plead guilty," and then throw himself upon the clemency of the court. Mercy cannot be exercised until guilt is confessed.

Similarly, God has to prove man guilty in order to save him. The first two chapters of Romans are God's fearful indictment against Gentile and Jew. He sums up the whole case by pronouncing both Jew and Gentile under sin, laying them prostrate and guilty before Himself, with every mouth stopped and every excuse silenced.

Then He begins to reveal the plan of salvation through the atonement and righteousness of Jesus Christ.

Once, in a French prison, a Russian prince, through the prerogative of Napoleon, was permitted to pardon any one convict. He proceeded to question the different men he met, with a view to finding someone worthy of his clemency. Every man he questioned professed to be entirely innocent, and, indeed, greatly wronged and unjustly punished.

At last, he found a man who frankly confessed his unworthiness, acknowledging that he deserved all the punishment he had received. The prince was deeply touched by his humility and penitence. "I have brought your forgiveness," he told him. In the name of your emperor, I pronounce you a free man. You are the only man I have found in all this place ready to acknowledge his guilt and take the place where mercy could be extended.

This is the place that God is bringing men to. When He gets them there, He loves to lift them up to His bosom and pronounce upon them, not the sentence of condemnation, but the word of acquittal and forgiveness.

In John Bunyan's beautiful allegory of Mansoul, we have an account of the surrender of the garrison to King Immanuel. The soldiers resisted as long as they could, but beleaguered and starving, they were finally compelled to give up the conflict and yield themselves to their conqueror.

The king's decree was that every one of them, with chains upon their necks, must come forth into his presence crying, "We are guilty and worthy of death." And so, in great humility and fear, they marched forth from the city gates and threw themselves at his feet. They expected the severest punishment, for they had resisted to the bitter end and knew that they deserved nothing but death.

But as soon as they had echoed their humble confession, King Immanuel ordered the herald to proclaim, in the hearing of all his camp, that they were freely pardoned through his mercy and restored to his favor. Their city would be rebuilt and become his own royal capital, and it would be treated with peculiar favor, and they themselves should be adopted as the children of the king.

The soldiers were overwhelmed with astonishment and burst into tears of gratitude and shouts of praise.

Yes, this is the glorious paradox of divine mercy. "God hath concluded all under sin, that he might have mercy upon all."

The passage before us unfolds, with extraordinary force and clearness, the principles of the divine salvation. It is called the righteousness of God.

We are so accustomed to think of redemption as an expedient for the relief of man that we quite forget its greater and more divine aspect as the revelation of the righteousness of God.

The purpose of Christ's work was not merely to relieve man from a dangerous situation, but to reveal God in the highest attitude and aspect of justice, wisdom and love, not only for His own glory, but also for the highest dignity and security of redeemed man. God has made the plan of salvation more a matter of justice and righteousness than of grace and mercy. All through the Epistle to the Romans, the term "righteousness" predominates in describing the plan of salvation.

This is the difference between Christianity and all human religions. Human religions try to bring God down to the level of man's sinfulness, adjusting the moral scale to the low standard of man's actual condition.

God's plan of salvation is just the opposite. It aims to bring man's condition up to the level of divine law. Not one principle of justice is compromised, not one jot or tittle of the law is modified or evaded. Every requirement of justice is met, and when man is saved, he is enabled to stand without a blush of shame and claim his acquittal from the very decree of eternal justice as much as from the gentle bosom of forgiving mercy.

I remember a noble friend of many years ago, a businessman of high standing among his fellows. I often used to mark his manly bearing, the high and noble dignity of his countenance, his walk and the profound respect in which he was held by all his acquaintances. One day I learned his secret.

He had failed in business a number of years before and was offered a settlement by his creditors that involved a compromise of his debts. This he would not accept, but asked only for time and opportunity to pay back every dollar, with interest. He went back to the struggle of life to do this and never ceased from his high purpose. At last he had redeemed his pledge and met the claims of every man to the last cent. Then he walked the streets of that city with the majesty of a king among men. He was not forgiven, he was justified.

This is what God aims to do in the plan of salvation. He does not want to pass over the transgressions of the sinner by a mere act of kindness. He wants us to know that every sin has been actually dealt with, punished and ended, and that we are in the same position with the law of God as if we had never sinned — as if we had kept every command of the law blamelessly. Through our great Substitute, sin has not only been met and punished, but, through His atonement, we are made blameless and the same as if we had suffered ourselves.

The term *justify* means to declare righteous. It does not necessarily imply that the one declared righteous *is* righteous. In fact, it is assumed, in the case of the sinner, that he *is not* righteous. It is the ungodly one whom God justifies, but he is recognized, not in himself, but in the person of his Substitute, the Lord Jesus Christ. Christ's righteousness is regarded as his; for Christ's sake, God treats the guilty one as though he were Christ.

Yes, the life which Jesus Christ laid down is accepted for our forfeited life, and the obedience which He rendered is accounted as our obedience. "[He was made] sin for us, who knew no sin; that we might be made the righteousness of God in Him" (2 Corinthians 5:21). And we sinners can look in the face of a Holy God and say, "There is therefore now no condemnation to them which are in Christ Jesus" (Romans 8:1). We can face the great accuser and cry, "Who is he that condemneth? It is Christ that died" (Romans 8:34). We may even face our conscience and the victims of our very crimes, and with hearts breaking with humble contrition, cry "Who shall lay any thing to the charge of God's elect? It is God that justifieth" (v. 33).

## The ground of justification

The ground of this righteousness is set forth by three terms that are very significant. The first is *redemption*, "the redemption that is in Christ Jesus."

This denotes a definite transaction through which we are purchased back from a condition of liability to punishment, through a price or ransom definitely paid.

The salvation of man is based upon a very specific transaction between the Father and the Son. It is based on a covenant of redemption entered into in the ages past and actually fulfilled by the Lord Jesus Christ when He became incarnate on earth and died on Calvary. The Father stipulated in this covenant that, for certain conditions, He would give to His Son the eternal salvation of His people. These conditions involved Jesus' perfect obedience, the offering up of His life on the cross and all the mediatorial acts which our Savior is now fulfilling.

These conditions have been absolutely fulfilled, and now as the completion of this transaction, God forgives the believer and saves the penitent, trusting soul. Therefore, we read, "If we confess our sins, he is faithful and just to forgive us our sins, and to cleanse us from all unrighteousness" (1 John 1:9). It is a matter of righteousness for Him to do so. Again, we are told, "[To] as many as received him, to them gave he [the right] to become the sons of God, even to them that believe on his name" (John 1:12). Thus, "we have redemption through his blood, the forgiveness of sins, according to the riches of his grace" (Ephesians 1:7).

The second of these terms is *propitiation*. This word literally means, covering. It is also used as a corresponding word in the Old Testament, to signify cleansing. The literal idea, however, is that of covering. It suggests the mercy seat in the tabernacle. The position of the mercy seat was strikingly significant of its spiritual reference. It was the covering of the ark. Underneath it, and within the ark, lay the tables of the law which man had broken and which witnessed against his sin.

Over the ark hovered the Shekinah, symbolical of God's all-seeing eye. That eye was looking down upon the ark. Had it seen only that broken law and the sin against which it testified, it could only have flashed its holy fires against the transgressors. It could not have rested in covenant love upon the worshipers in that sacred place.

But it did not see the sin at all, for between the ark and the Shekinah was the mercy seat, the covering lid of pure gold always sprinkled with the blood of atonement. God saw only the blood, and it covered the sin. As a result, we read such words as these: "Blessed are they whose iniquities are forgiven, and whose sins are covered" (Romans 4:7). "He hath not beheld iniquity in Jacob, neither hath he seen perverseness in Israel" (Numbers 23:21). "[Christ] is the propitiation for our sins: and not for ours only, but also for the sins of the whole world" (1 John 2:2).

The third term used is *his blood*. Of course this refers to Christ's death. The blood is the life, and the offering of Christ's blood expressed His vicarious sacrifice for sin. The ransom was His life, the propitiation is His blood. He has stood between us and the just consequences of our guilt, and "The Lord hath laid on him the iniquity of us all" (Isaiah 53:6). "Who his own self bare our sins in his own body on the tree, that we, being dead to sins, should live unto righteousness: by whose stripes ye were healed" (1 Peter 2:24).

This is the core of Christianity. This is the essence of the gospel. This is the ground of our justification. God has set forth Jesus Christ so emphatically that His great atonement cannot be misunderstood or evaded by any honest mind. He is the propitiation through His blood. By Him God can "declare his righteousness for the remission of sins that are past, through the forbearance of God; . . . that he might be just, and the justifier of him which believeth in Jesus."

### The efficacy of His atonement

"For the remission of sins that are past, through the forbearance of God." The language here is very expressive, and it intimates that in the past, and up to the time of Christ's death, God was forbearing with sin, but it was not settled for.

There are two Greek words used, expressive of the two thoughts that stand forth here in bold relief. One is *paresis*, the other *aphesis*. *Paresis* means to pass by; *aphesis*, to put away. Under the Old Testament, it was *paresis*; under the New it is *aphesis*. Then, it was forbearance, now it is remission. Then, God overlooked sin, not lightly, nor capriciously, but in view of the settlement that was to be made by Christ on Calvary and which was recognized as already accomplished through "the Lamb slain from the foundation of the world" (Revelation 13:8). The ransom was not literally paid, but God dealt with men in forbearance and in anticipation of the coming atonement.

Christ had, as it were, given His promissory note for the payment of the ransom, and God accepted it and dealt with believers under the old covenant on the assurance that it would be paid. Christ made good that promissory note on Calvary, and thus sin was taken out of the way, nailed to His cross, and the full efficacy of His atonement became real. Sin was now cancelled, annihilated.

Christ had come to finish transgression, to make an end of sin, to bring in everlasting righteousness. We who accept the Lord Jesus are not only taken on probation, and dealt with as objects of forbearance, but we are wholly justified, eternally saved and received into the fellowship and communion of God, even as His own beloved Son, in whom we are accepted.

Jesus said:

> *He that heareth my word, and believeth on him that sent me, hath everlasting life, and shall not come into con-*

*demnation; but is passed from death unto life ( John 5:24).*

*My sheep hear my voice, and I know them, and they follow Me. And I give unto them eternal life; and they shall never perish, neither shall any man pluck them out of my hand ( John 10:27–28).*

The work of Jesus Christ is complete, final, eternal. "By one offering he hath perfected forever them that are sanctified" (Hebrews 10:14). "Now once in the end of the world hath he appeared to put away sin by the sacrifice of himself." "And unto them that look for him shall he appear the second time without sin unto salvation" (Hebrews 9:26, 28).

Is not this a glorious redemption, a divine foundation, a strong consolation, a Rock of Ages? Is not this a better resting place for your confidence and hope than all your transitory feelings and variable experiences? Is not this a blessed place to rest when the brain gets clouded, the heart gets sad and cold and the adversary hurls his fiery darts into the self-accusing conscience?

Well do I remember a dear old saint who had led a number of people to Christ. But as her sun began to do down and clouds gathered around her horizon, her brain grew weak, her faith became dimmed and she thought she was no longer useful to Jesus Christ and that He no longer wanted her. How sweet it was to tell her that her salvation rested upon the immutable Word of God. She was safe in Jesus Christ, the Rock of Ages, and nothing could ever shake that foundation!

Let us be sure that we are anchored fast to this eternal Rock — our Redeemer and Lord Jesus Christ.

## The terms of righteousness

"Being justified freely by His grace." The verse expresses almost a redundancy, for *freely* and *grace* mean the same. But the design of the writer is to convey the idea with all possible emphasis. This salvation, all the way through, is the gift of God. We cannot earn it, deserve it or work it out ourselves. We must receive it from beginning to end directly from our Father's hands on equal terms of mercy and personal worthlessness. Our works, experiences and usefulness have nothing whatever to do with securing our salvation.

I have no more right to my salvation because I have been serving Jesus 35 years, than that poor man who last night received Jesus in the city mission, stepping out of a life of reeking uncleanness. When I stand in the presence of my Lord, my only plea must be:

> Saved by grace alone,
>   This is all my plea —
> Jesus died for all mankind
>   And Jesus died for me.

There is no difference in the standing of any of us at the gateway of life. "All have sinned, and come short of the glory of God; Being justified freely by his grace . . ." (Romans 3:23–24). Whatever else we have along with this — whatever of holiness or usefulness God has permitted any of us to enjoy — this also is through the riches of His grace. "What hast thou that thou didst not receive?" (1 Corinthians 7:7). Even Paul had to say, in speaking of his salvation, "I obtained mercy," and then he added of his subsequent career, "The grace of our Lord was exceeding abundant with faith and love which is in Christ Jesus" (1 Timothy 1:14).

While it is true that there is a great difference at the end, there is none at the beginning. On equal terms we enter the gates of mercy, all alike condemned, and then we are permitted, in the great goodness of God, to strive for the crown of recompense and press toward the goal in the race for victory.

It is just the same as if, in some great public school, free admission should be given to all who applied, irrespective of their personal circumstances and merit. After they are admitted freely to the school, however, there are prizes given to the students according to their diligence and proficiency in the various studies.

So God takes us all in as helpless, worthless sinners. After we enter the school of Christ as the beneficiaries of His grace, we are invited and permitted to press forward to the higher rewards which He offers to the diligent and faithful.

But even the power to gain the reward and strive for the mastery is still the gift of grace and infinite mercy. And so it is all of grace, through the purchase of Christ's precious blood and the gift of the Father's sovereign love.

## Received by faith

"The righteousness of God which is by faith of Jesus Christ unto all and upon all them that believe: for there is no difference." This is the principle underlying the whole gospel system. Every blessing must be received by faith. This is the only way in which a gift can be received. There is no merit in an act of faith. It is simply taking what God gives with thanks and trust.

Faith is certainly a blessed act, because when our hearts receive the love and grace of God, faith has exercised a blessed influence on our lives and characters. But in itself faith is not a work of merit but simply the means by which we receive what God has to give.

Note also that it is the "law of faith" (Romans 3:27). It is the principle on which God is acting with men. "Without faith it is impossible to please [God]" (Hebrews 11:6a). Let us realize faith's essential importance in our own lives and accept it as the principle and law of our life, as it is the law of God's administration for sinful mankind.

God has the boundless riches of His grace for the most lost and sinful, if they will only accept the gift and receive it by simple trust. But they can be lost by unbelief much more certainly than by the darkest crime of which human nature is capable.

In order to teach his peasantry the lesson of trusting God, an English landlord once offered on a certain morning to pay the debts of all his tenantry if they would bring him a statement of what they owed and accept as a gift his generous bounty.

The day came. People gathered in curious knots around the street near the landlord's office, wondering what it all meant. They could not understand such liberal generosity. They waited for someone to enter and prove that the landlord really meant what he said. Then they also would go in for their share. But the morning wore on, and no one was willing to step forward.

At last an aged couple tottered up the street, bent on reaching the landlord's office. The people crowded around them and said eagerly, "Now be sure to hurry through and tell us all about it!"

The landlord received the old couple very kindly,

looked over their statement, agreed gladly to pay the debts and then asked them if there was anything more he could do for their comfort. He said that he had a certain sum of money that he intended to spend in this way, but none of the people seemed to want it. So he gave the old couple enough to buy a little cottage and to supply the needs of their closing days. They poured out their thanks with tears of joy.

When the couple arose to go, the lord detained them a few moments, chatting pleasantly with them, until the clock struck 12. Then he arose, opened the door for them and bade them goodbye. As the couple tottered feebly down the steps, the crowd eagerly pressed about them, asking, "Did he really pay your debts?" "Did he mean it?" The old people looked at them with astonishment in their faces and said, "Why, of course!"

The people now pressed toward the door, anxious to enter. But by then the landlord was leaving. "Good afternoon, neighbors!" he said, bowing. "I am sorry you were so late, but another engagement calls me away. The time of my offer has expired. Your opportunity has passed."